James L. Sullivan

LifeWay Press
Nashville, Tennessee

Copyright 1955 Broadman Press, renewed 1983

All rights reserved

Revised 1969
Reprinted 1975, 1977, 1978, 1979, 1980, 1982,
1985, 1986, 1988, 1990, 1992, 1995, 1997
Commemorative Edition 2001
Reprinted 2002

No part of this work may be reproduced or transmitted
in any form or by any means, electronic or mechanical,
including photocopying and recording, or by any
information storage or retrieval system, except as
may be expressly permitted in writing by the publisher.
Requests for permission should be addressed in writing to
LifeWay Press, One LifeWay Plaza, Nashville, TN 37234-0175.

ISBN 0-7673-2005-0

Dewey Decimal Classification 262.7
Subject Heading: Church Membership

To order additional copies of this resource:
WRITE LifeWay Church Resources Customer Service,
One LifeWay Plaza; Nashville, TN 37234-0113;
FAX (615) 251-5933; PHONE 1-800-458-2772;
EMAIL *customerservice@lifeway.com;*
order ONLINE at *www.lifeway.com;* or
visit the LifeWay Christian Store serving you.

Printed in the United States of America

Leadership and Adult Publishing
LifeWay Church Resources
One LifeWay Plaza
Nashville, Tennessee 37234-0175

When you consider the number of books published, few can claim the status of being a classic. This book can. For that reason, LifeWay Church Resources is pleased to offer this commemorative edition of *Your Life and Your Church* by Dr. James L. Sullivan. This book was first released in 1955 and continues to be one of the finest resources available for churches to use in guiding new members into active Christian discipleship.

Churches that have a practical plan, provide a time and place, and offer good resources, bring new members into the full benefit of the fellowship which they have joined. This book can be used in groups or in personal conferences with new members. You may want to offer *Your Life and Your Church* during a regular discipleship training time. Whenever it is scheduled, it should be at a time most convenient for those participating.

If you have used this book before, you will find that the only change in the text is in the updating of organization titles. The principles Dr. Sullivan first presented have not changed and remain as valid today as they were in 1955. As you use this book as a single resource or a supplement for training new members, you will find it to be effective and useful for believers. It will help them now and will become a reference for them throughout their lifelong Christian journey.

Dr. James L. Sullivan

About the Author

James L. Sullivan served Southern Baptists as president of the Sunday School Board, now LifeWay Christian Resources, Nashville, Tennessee from 1953-1975.

His interest in church work dates back to his childhood in Tylertown, Mississippi, where he could hardly wait until his ninth birthday to join the Junior B.Y.P.U. He was converted and baptized at the age of 11, and participated in all of the affairs of his church during his junior and intermediate years.

Ordained by the Tylertown Baptist Church in 1930, he has served as pastor of Baptist churches at Boston and Beaver Dam in Kentucky, Ripley and Nashville (Belmont Heights) in Tennessee, Clinton and Brookhaven in Mississippi, and Abilene (First) in Texas.

Dr. Sullivan continues to be active in his church, First Baptist Church, Nashville, TN. He speaks at LifeWay functions and occasionally at state and Southern Baptist Convention meetings. He has written numerous articles for Sunday School and Discipleship Training periodicals.

He has also served the denomination as president of the Tennessee Baptist Convention and as a trustee of Southern Baptist Theological Seminary, Union University, Hardin-Simmons University, Midstate Baptist Hospital, Hendrick Memorial Hospital, the Sunday School Board; vice-president of the Baptist World Alliance; chairman of Division of Evangelism and Education, Baptist World Alliance; and president of the Southern Baptist Convention.

Preface

This book was written for new church members. It does not propose to deal exhaustively with, or delve deeply into, Baptist doctrines and procedures. Rather, it is a summary of all that Baptists are and believe. Brevity is not only desired, but demanded here.

This manuscript was prepared with the desire and design of meeting a specific need in the churches and especially in the lives of new converts. It attempts to describe the relation of the new convert to the church with which he has recently become affiliated. It tries to help him analyze his own experience of conversion, become more familiar with the principal doctrines of Baptists, and find his place of happy service in the everyday activities of the church through its organizations and worship services.

The entire presentation is given from a pastor's point of view. Let it be hoped that pastors throughout the Southern Baptist Convention territory will accept the challenge to teach this book with regularity and zeal to all new church members.

Knowing that Baptists have no church hierarchy to determine and announce the doctrines of their faith, a writer must of necessity present those teachings which are most prevalently held by the thousands of independent Baptist churches in the Southern Baptist territory. Who has the authority or dares to assume to be a mouthpiece or spokesman for Baptists? Baptist churches are independent bodies. On many issues there are free discussions and varied opinions. On the great fundamentals of the faith, however, they are united almost to a church and to a man. On lesser matters which are not "points of fellowship," Baptists enjoy and give great liberty of thought, action, and practice. When all is said and done, the apparent differences among Baptist churches are not so much conflicts in points of doctrine as they are variations in predominant emphases and programs.

It is hoped that this book will be received in the spirit in which it is given—that of real love and a prayer that God may use every page to help new church members become firmly fixed in the faith and useful in church life as they grow and develop into strong "fellow helpers to the truth."

James Sullivan

SUGGESTED OBJECTIVES FOR NEW CHURCH MEMBER TRAINING

In New Member Training a church is concerned with both new Christians and transfer members. Though needs may vary with different individuals, the basic objective of training is the same for all new members in both groups. It is to lead each new member to make the commitment to Christ and the church and to strive diligently for Christian maturity as called for in the New Testament. More specifically it is:

1. To help each new member understand and reaffirm his conversion experience and his commitment to Christ and the church.

2. To help each new member understand and accept the privileges and responsibilities of membership in the church.

3. To help each new member appropriate the resources of the Christian life and become a growing part of the Christian fellowship through involvement in the life of the church during and beyond the training period.

Some churches plan New Member Training for new Christians only, assuming that new members transferring their letters do not need it. A careful study of the needs of transfer members indicates that most of them need training as much as new Christians, some even more. Two factors are involved. First, many transfer members come not only bringing a letter but also recommitting a life, having been inactive in their church for a long period of time. They need badly to review the fundamentals of Christian faith. Then, much of this training has to do with the life and ministry of the local church; and no matter how one may have been involved in his former church, he still needs basic training in his new church.

However, there are exceptions, and occasionally a church receives a new member whose needs cannot be met by participation in the regular training program. In such cases, the church will use good judgment in adjusting its plan to meet specific personal needs.

1. The Meaning of Your Christian Experience 11
2. The Meaning of Church Membership 25
3. You and Your Church 41
4. Your Stewardship 53
5. Your Testimony 67
6. Your Home and Your Church 79
7. Your All for Christ 91

Teaching Helps 104

Christian Growth Study Plan 112

Chapter 1

Your Life & Your Church

THE MEANING OF YOUR CHRISTIAN EXPERIENCE

You are now a member of the church. Miraculous things have occurred recently in your inmost being. You have trusted Christ. That faith in Him as personal Savior has brought you salvation. Your salvation has brought happiness and a sense of victory.

Things will never be the same again. As a Christian you now rejoice in God's sweet forgiveness. You delight in fellowship with Christian people. You thrill over happy thoughts of the promises of God. Life's directions have been reversed. Life's motives have been revised. As a church member you have accepted obligations which you had never dreamed of assuming before you became a Christian.

You expect great accomplishments in your own life. This is as it should be. God also expects wonderful things from you. You are in His spiritual army now. As a member of His church, you have joined hands and hearts with the mightiest forces in the world. Your life will help lift the very moral tone of the world in your time. Your community will be a better place because you have come to know Jesus and to follow Him as Master.

In order that you might better understand and appreciate the significant things which have recently happened in your life, the first chapter discusses the meaning of your Christian experience. In this way you can recall and relive recent spiritual experiences which are meaningful and eternal. You can also understand the lost and tragic condition of your own soul before you came to know Jesus. You can more deeply appreciate the mercy of a loving God. You can better know about the cleansing power of a mighty Saviour who rescued you from your sins and saved you for service and eternity.

There are some things about the experience of salvation which the Christian can never understand fully this side of heaven. For instance, God never tells just how the blood of Jesus Christ erases the sin stains of one who trusts in Him. Salvation is based on faith, nevertheless. It is not determined by knowledge. One can enjoy salvation fully even though he does not understand it completely.

God planned salvation. Jesus purchased it with His blood. Man must accept Christ with a personal faith. Heaven is the future home of the Christian. These and many other things the Christian can know positively. These truths which are understandable are the things which are discussed in this book. The things that are beyond human understanding now shall be fully known when heaven becomes your home.

1. Your Life Without Christ

Let us analyze the spiritual state of a lost soul. It may well be a study of your life before Jesus came into it. A glance at the things from which you have been saved will make you more grateful for the matchless things Christ has done for you.

A sinner's life is one of tragedy and despair. A close study will show that the lost person's life is:

(1) Incomplete.—God has drawn a blueprint of His eternal plan of the ages. In that plan God has a purpose for every life. The lost man's life is shaped by selfishness, not by divine design. Life to the non-Christian is, therefore, woefully incomplete. It is as incomplete as the human body without blood, or stairs without a house. It is a life out of touch. It is a woeful misfit in God's wonderful world.

Christless lives are never full and well-rounded. Sinners seek but never find. They quest but never discover. They yearn for spiritual things but never come to possess them. Never do they sense achievement or accomplishment. They feel that they are journeying but can never arrive. A sense of inadequacy possesses them.

The purposes of life are tragically unfulfilled when sinful men do not receive Christ. The secret of successful living goes undiscovered as long as they remain outside of Christ.

Chapter 1 *The Meaning of Your Christian Experience*

(2) Unhappy.—No unhappiness can compare with that of a sinner. With stained hands and a confused mind, he lives in a state of utter discontent. His straying feet and condemning conscience produce a burdened heart. His is the very essence of wretched living. Paul describes him with the words ". . . dead in trespasses and sins . . . the course of this world . . . the lusts of our flesh . . . by nature the children of wrath" (Eph. 2:1-3). Every saint today was at one time a sinner with awful unhappiness in his soul. Does not the Bible say, "All have sinned, and come short of the glory of God" (Rom. 3:23)?

Jesus wants people to possess true happiness. He Himself began the Sermon on the Mount by promising that he would provide happiness to His followers if they would meet certain spiritual conditions. "Blessed" means happy (Matt. 5:2-11). All men yearn to be happy. The sinner can never realize his dream of happiness until he trusts Jesus as Saviour. Jesus is the only source of real heart happiness.

(3) Lost.—The word God uses to describe the condition of a sinner without Christ is "lost." What a vivid description to anyone who has ever been lost! With jumbled-up thoughts and a jaded sense of direction the sinner is frantic and desperate. That is always true of a lost man. It is a sad condition in human living. No wonder the Bible says plainly, "The way of transgressors is hard" (Prov. 13:15). The sinner's way is harder by far than the way of the Christian. It is true at each step of the way in human living. Who wants to live a lost life?

(4) Condemned.—The sinner is not only unhappy, but he is under condemnation. "The wages of sin is death" (Rom. 6:23). Held responsible for his every sin, he finds the burdening load too heavy. His sin debts are many. He cannot pay them alone. The price can be paid only with blood. The Bible says, "Without shedding of blood is no remission" (Heb. 9:22). That stern fact makes it impossible for him to purchase his own freedom and live. He has refused the only possible pardon by his rejection of Christ. He stands condemned as a guilty sinner before the very God of heaven. Never was a criminal under surer condemnation in any court than a sinner is before the righteous God. He is condemned before the Judge who knows all and in a court from which there is no appeal.

(5) Helpless.—Trusting in himself alone, the sinner is helpless to cleanse, lift, or deliver himself. One cannot change or purity life by a mere wish. The sinner is unable to meet any of his deep spiritual needs alone. Only Christ can help. Without Christ the sinner is helpless indeed. If the sinner refuses what Christ gives, he is not only without help, but without hope.

2. God's Concern for Your Need

Some people care little about the sinner's condition. God's care is exceedingly deep. He is anxious that every lost soul be won. If God had not cared for you, your plight would have been hopeless indeed.

(1) God's compassion.—Have you ever tried to imagine what the world would be like if God did not care? Suppose the sun refused to shine, or the law of gravity failed to operate. How long could man have survived had God not cared enough to make provision for all of his material and spiritual needs?

God could doubtless have found many excuses had He sought to rid Himself of a rebellious mankind. With all God has to do in operating a universe, it would seem that He is too busy to concern Himself with the problems and sins of any one man upon earth. God's heart, however, is not like man's heart. Nothing takes precedence over God's love and compassion for mankind. He made the world, but He made it for man.

The compassion of God's heart for wayward mankind is expressed in the lament of Jesus as He wept, "O Jerusalem, Jerusalem, . . . how often would I have gathered thy children together, as a hen doth gather her brood under her wings, and ye would not!" (Luke 13:34). That lament of our Lord reveals the heart of God as He yearned for lost souls and rebellious lives. God's heart was like Christ's heart. Compassion for a wayward man was real and deep.

The chaplain of a penitentiary conducted the funeral service of a convict who had been killed. The criminal had been a very dangerous character.

Chapter 1 *The Meaning of Your Christian Experience*

The chaplain had phoned the father to ask suggestions about the funeral service only to receive the reply: "Do anything you like with him. It does not matter with me." His mother, divorced from that unconcerned father, gave a similar response with the words: "I never cared too much about him. It doesn't matter what you do with him now. Bury him when and where you please."

At a lonely graveside in a potter's field the chaplain stood with aching heart to speak some appropriate words at the last rite of a notorious and murdered criminal. The preacher and a couple of armed guards were the only persons present who were not clothed in prison stripes. Throughout the brief service one deep emotion was surging through the preacher's soul. It was expressed in the words: "Nobody cared. Father did not love him. Mother was not concerned about him. No one bothered to give him help and guidance. Little did anyone care about what he did or did not do. Perhaps this potter's grave is his fate because no one cared."

While a mother's love is usually one of the greatest things in the world, it sometimes fails. Greater than any parent's love is the concern of the Heavenly Father for the people of the earth. It never fails. Human love at its best becomes insignificant when compared with the magnificent love of the mighty God of heaven. His concern is so great that it will melt the heart of any wayfaring sinner who pauses to meditate on such love.

The Bible says, "While we were yet sinners, Christ died for us" (Rom. 5:8). What truth! Jesus did not come to the earth to die for us because we were righteous. He came to live and die for us because we were unworthy sinners. Such deep compassion cannot be fathomed or understood.

(2) *God's promise.*–Long before Jesus came, God made the promise that a Messiah would be sent to provide man's salvation. For generations man dreamed of that hope and prayed for the day when God's Son would come.

The promise of that deliverer was first made in Eden immediately after the fall of man. It was with the prophecy that a descendant would be born of woman who would bruise the serpent's head (Gen. 3:15). Through the generations prophets came to remind men of that blessed hope. One of the greatest of those recorded reminders is Isaiah 53. It described Jesus accurately and vividly many centuries before his birth.

The promise to send the Saviour was something God could not forget. It was always on His heart. In the fullness of time God would keep that promise and man's deepest spiritual needs would be met. God's promise was surer than any man's bonded guarantee.

(3) God's gift.—At Bethlehem Jesus came in fulfillment of God's promise to send a Saviour for man. God kept his promise fully. Jesus came as God's gift of love and salvation. The coming of Christ illustrated and proved the compassionate heart of God. God's love was also illustrated by the depth to which Jesus was willing to go that men might be lifted from condemnation and sin to the high rewards of heaven.

In Old Testament times men offered lambs and bullocks in sacrifice for their transgressions. The day came when God sent Jesus to be the "Lamb of God" (John 1:29). He was without spot or blemish (1 Peter 1:19) and would die to take away the sins of believing men through all the ages to come.

It is important for us to remember that salvation was furnished by God and not by man. It was God's love and compassion that made the difference. God took every initiative in man's salvation. It was God who gave His holy Word, the Bible. It was God who sent His prophets to proclaim their messages with fiery words which would melt the hearts of hardened men. God called His preachers. He established His churches. He has guided the destinies of men so that they would hear the message of redemption. Today God is following the same course in reaching down to rescue mankind. He provides the Holy Spirit today to point men to the one way of hope.

Jesus is wholly undeserved by man. Salvation itself cannot be earned or purchased. It is "the gift of God" (Rom. 6:23). It is free. That is what we mean when we speak of salvation by grace (Eph. 2:8). Salvation is undeserved, but God gave it. It cannot be borrowed or bartered. It cannot be possessed in any other way but by faith in Christ (Acts 4:12).

Chapter 1 *The Meaning of Your Christian Experience*

3. Your Salvation Through Christ

The hour you believed is a blessed hour. It will always be remembered by you. It was truly an individual experience. Yet it was in some ways very much like every Christian's conversion. Each conversion is different in some detail from any other experience of salvation. While all conversion experiences differ, however, there are basic similarities which are universally true to all human experiences with God.

An 11-year-old boy had gone to church one Sunday morning. He had listened to the preacher with unusual interest and concern. The sermon, while not unusually outstanding, had dug deeply into his own young heart and made him feel his personal need of God. Being aware of no one about him, that boy felt that the preacher's message was directed personally to his own listening heart. He deeply desired to know God in his own heart and life.

The hymn of invitation was sung at the close of the sermon. The young boy did not respond by going forward at once to make public profession. His delay was caused by question marks and doubt. He experienced desire and hesitation. He felt the urge to go. He also felt the urge not to go. God was wooing him on. The devil was pulling hard to keep him back. The invitation hymn was finished. There was no decisive decision or action. The church service closed without one single addition or profession.

Unlike many of the other days, the young boy went home burdened in soul for himself. He spent most of the afternoon in prayer. It was shortly before the evening services that he gained joy instead of sadness. He felt God come into his heart. His burdens were rolled away. His spirit was filled with a song.

This young fellow went to church telling others of his newfound friend and his newborn life. At the evening worship hour he moved hastily forward at the very first word of the first hymn of invitation to relate his experience of conversion and request baptism and church membership. He had come to know the Lord in faith, and he knew that he knew. God has been near and dear to his heart from that eventful day until the present hour.

Analyzing that individual experience we see some fundamental things which are true in every man's conversion.

(1) Conviction.—The Holy Spirit has a number of things to do on earth. One of those tasks is to make the sinner conscious of his sin and aware of his soul's need. Until God's Spirit convicts the sinner, he may pride himself in his goodness. Frequently, he feels that he is better than most of the people of his town.

When the Holy Spirit touches the sinner's heart and reveals the infinite purity of God, it is only natural that he then cries out in helpless concern for God to do something about his soul's needs which have become so great. Conviction shows him the blackness of his own soul. The Spirit makes him feel a need in his own heart. He gives the sinner a yearning for deliverance. The experience of conviction is not pleasant. It is necessary, however, for one to be willing to be purged and cleansed. Until one is aware that he is sick he will not cry out for a physician. Until one senses his need for God he will not seek or receive an experience with God.

The fact that the Holy Spirit convicts of sin is shown clearly in John (John 16:8). Conviction is the first step toward righteousness.

(2) Repentance and faith.—One's cry for help results from his repentance. Repentance is a sense of sin, a sorrow for sin, and a willingness to be separated from that sin. Repentance is also a necessary step in conversion. That is why Jesus said, "Except ye repent, ye shall all likewise perish" (Luke 13:3). The twin of repentance is faith. Repentance and faith must always go together. They are as inseparable as two sides of the same coin. When a person repents, he trusts. When he trusts, he has repented. Soul sorrow drives a person to despair and leads him to cast himself on Jesus. It makes one willing to break with sins which have dominated his life. It means the placing of oneself in Christ's hands for fullest usefulness and service. Faith is the casting of oneself on Jesus that the entire life might be used and the full rewards of heaven might be received.

(3) Conversion.—The moment you believed, Jesus became your Saviour. He forgave all your sins and removed them "as far as the east is from the west" (Psalm 103:12). Salvation became full and

complete in your own life. Jesus purchased your full pardon. His death on the cross paid the full debt for every sin of your life. His physical death made your spiritual life possible. That experience is called conversion. Telling others of that sin and conversion is called confession. That, too, is important to Jesus (Rom. 10:10).

When one trusts Christ, the salvation he receives is for eternity. By faith he is born again. That faith is from above. His spiritual birth makes him a child of God. Nothing in the future can sever that relation of sonship to God. The Christian's life is an "everlasting life." It is an "eternal salvation." There is nothing fleeting or temporary about the soul salvation which Jesus gives. God is the keeper (John 10:28). How wonderful that fact is! Man cannot save himself. Man cannot keep himself. God can and does both through Christ.

On the cross Jesus died for human sin. His death atoned for sin. Having paid fully for the penalty for sin, there is no occasion on which another person can be called forth to suffer again for that same transgression. In no court in the land is it expected that a man suffer twice for the same transgression. Jesus suffered and died to pay fully for human transgression. There will never be an occasion when a believer will be called upon to suffer for the selfsame sin for which Jesus died. Salvation, therefore, is eternal for the Christian. God assures it.

4. Your Growth in Discipleship

(1) Spiritual birth.—The conversion experience is not the end of one's walk with God. It is the beginning. It is the first step, not the last.

Your conversion experience was at the beginning of your spiritual life. Just as an infant has much room to grow, you as a new Christian are also expected to grow. The conversion experience was your new birth. It made you a child of God. The rest of your life you are to grow in grace and in the knowledge of the Lord and Saviour, Jesus Christ. Growth must have a beginning. With the Christian that beginning is conversion.

(2) Spiritual growth.—Many factors contribute to Christian growth. It is not a matter of accident. It is by systematic training and

development. The Christian graces (Gal. 5:22-24) characterize the child of God as he grows and develops with every passing day. Just as the athlete struggles hard to be victorious, so must the Christian endeavor conscientiously to live a triumphant life.

In order for one to grow there must be a complete yielding to the Master. Jesus not only wants to be the Saviour of the soul; He wants also to be Master of the life. If a branch is to bear fruit, it must remain close to the vine and receive strength from it. If we are to be fruitful in Christian living, we must stay close to Jesus and receive fruit-bearing strength from Him.

Many times Jesus allows us to suffer life's hardships in order to purge us of worldliness, strengthen us for service, or to teach His nearness. In the early days the disciples vainly wished that they could be lifted out of the persecuting world the moment of conversion. Jesus said of them, "I pray not that thou shouldest take them out of the world" (John 17:15). In other words, Jesus wanted to leave his followers amid the obstacles of life in order that their good works might declare their faith and give testimony which the world needed to see and hear.

(3) Spiritual maturity.—It is a glorious thing to see one who has become a giant in the faith. Such spiritual development does not happen in a day. Just as strong bodies result from years of rigid exercise and rugged control, so Christian strength is the result of long years of walking with God in deep devotion and sacrificial discipleship.

Occasionally Christians do become dwarfed. They come to neglect church attendance. They become unconcerned about their prayer lives. They are in effect spiritual midgets. Few things afford sadder sights in God's eyes. While they have been Christians for many years, they are essentially the same size spiritually that they were on the day they made their professions of faith. Tragedy of tragedies! God never intended it.

If there is anything Jesus likes to see in us, it is childlikeness. If there is anything he detests, it is childishness. The Master's appeal for Christian maturity is seen in many places in the Bible. He wants us to grow strong. He yearns for us to be strong.

Chapter 1 *The Meaning of Your Christian Experience*

If we yield our lives to Him, He will use them fully. He will mature us by experiences through which He will lead us. He will then give back to us more of ourselves than we gave to Him at the beginning. One cannot sacrifice permanently when he places his life in the Master's hands. The principle of Christian compensation is illustrated in the life of the lad (John 6) who yielded his loaves and fishes to Jesus. With the yielded loaves and fishes the multitudes were fed. The same principle still applies. The more we give to Christ, the more of life He returns to us.

You will only be converted once. The salvation you received at conversion was for eternity. The years, however, provide you with many spiritual experiences which will lift you to higher levels of thinking and serving. The meaningful experience of conversion will be fresh throughout your lifetime if you share it with others. The more the story of Jesus is told, the fresher your own Christian experience will remain. Christian experience is something you can give and share. But you do not lose anything by sharing. Give much! Much will come back to you.

SUMMARY OF CHAPTER 1
The Meaning of Your Christian Experience

Introduction

1. *Your Life Without Christ*
    (1) Incomplete (John 10:10)
    (2) Unhappy (Isa. 6:5)
    (3) Lost (John 3:36)
    (4) Condemned (John 3:18)
    (5) Helpless (Matt. 15:25)

2. *God's Concern for Your Need*
    (1) God's compassion (Ezek. 33:11)
    (2) God's promise (Matt. 1:21)
    (3) God's gift (John 3:16)

3. *Your Salvation Through Christ*
    (1) Conviction (John 16:8)
    (2) Repentance and faith (Luke 13:3; Acts 16:31)
    (3) Conversion (Matt. 18:3)

4. *Your Growth in Discipleship*
    (1) Spiritual birth (John 3:3)
    (2) Spiritual growth (2 Peter 3:18)
    (3) Spiritual maturity (Heb. 5:12-14)

Chapter 1 *The Meaning of Your Christian Experience*

QUESTIONS FOR DISCUSSION

Chapter 1

1. Discuss God's love for all sinners.
2. Tell how God proved His love to sinners.
3. Relate your own experience of conversion.
4. What can you do to hasten your Christian growth?
5. Discuss some ways by which the world can come to know that Jesus is your Master as well as your Saviour.

COMMITMENT

For the New Church Member

I have trusted Christ as my Saviour. Feeling that He wants to use my life because He has saved my soul, I do here and now yield myself fully to Him. With His help I will follow Him faithfully as long as I live.

(Signed) _____

Chapter 2

Your Life & Your Church

THE MEANING OF CHURCH MEMBERSHIP

Church membership is the natural thing for a Christian. The believer's first desire is to please Jesus. When the Bible said, "Christ also loved the church, and gave himself for it" (Eph. 5:25), it described Christ's affection and also characterized Christ's followers. A Christian loves what Christ loved. One cannot please Jesus by neglecting His church. It would not be natural or possible for one to love Jesus and yet be indifferent to the institution which He loved so devotedly and for which He died so sacrificially. Because Jesus loved the church, everyone who loves Christ will come to love His church also. That is why the church means so much to the Christian. Jesus' affection for the church shapes His followers' devotion to it.

Church membership means more than one can at first imagine. Each member should seek to honor Christ in every church relationship. One who does will be amazed at the happy surprises awaiting him. A believer will never find his place of fullest usefulness or deepest happiness outside of the church. Jesus planned it that way. The Christian's greatest needs are met through the church in which he serves. His greatest means of service is through the church.

To understand the church better we need to study what it is and for what it stands.

1. The Church a Divine Institution

(1) Jesus established the church.—The church has a holy mission and a sacred message. It is not just another earthly organization. It is ever living and growing. It is more of an organism than an

organization. It is alive. Hear Jesus say, "Upon this rock I will build my church" (Matt. 16:18). It is divine in its origin. Christ is its head (Eph. 5:23). It is enlarging in its influence. It has a mission which is both mighty and eternal.

There has been questioning about the exact time that the church was started. Let no discussions hide the fact that Jesus did establish it. He evidently began it before the day of Pentecost. It seems certain that the church was begun simply when Jesus called together his baptized disciples for the purpose of uniting their efforts in the furtherance of His wonderful work on earth. That the church was in existence before Pentecost is proved by Jesus' instruction to His disciples, "Tell it unto the church" (Matt. 18:17). These words were spoken long before Pentecost. Jesus would hardly have recommended that a matter be referred to a nonexistent body. While Jesus empowered the church with His Spirit at Pentecost, He actually began it during His earthly ministry. It will continue until Jesus comes again.

(2) The Great Commission given to the church.—The Great Commission was given to the church near the time of Jesus' departure from earth and His return to heaven. It was a commandment given by the Master to His church. That is why we look upon baptism as a church ordinance. Here is the reason also for considering missions to be a binding church obligation. Christ's work is too big for any individual regardless of genius or wealth. Individuals die. The church lives on and on. Jesus ordered the assembled body of baptized believers to carry forward the great work of making disciples and baptizing them. It is an assignment we are to carry into all the world and into every age. We must ever accept that missionary responsibility as a binding church duty. The so-called church that is antimissionary or "o-missionary" is unchristian. Jesus' words were clear as He said, "Go ye therefore, and teach all nations, baptizing them in the name of the Father, and of the Son, and the Holy Ghost; teaching them to observe all things whatsoever I have commanded you" (Matt. 28:19-20). To be missionary is mandatory.

Jesus' commandment has not been obeyed fully until we have taught men "to obey" His commandments as well as to trust His saving power. That is why the church must teach His Word so vigorously and persistently to all of its members after they have been won and baptized. Our task is incomplete until men hear, believe, and obey.

(3) Victory promised the church.—The growth of the churches from insignificant little bodies in New Testament days to tremendous instruments of power in our world today indicates that Jesus is keeping His promise and guarantee of ultimate victory. The "gates of hell shall not prevail" (Matt. 16:18) over those divinely guided and guarded groups of servants who render Him service. Christ has guaranteed their permanence and growth. They may be persecuted, but they cannot be destroyed. They may face hardships, but in the end they will be triumphant. Christ has ordered it.

2. *The Membership of the Church*

(1) The New Testament meaning of the church.—The predominant Bible meaning of the word "church" is assembly or congregation. Expressions like "the churches of Galatia" (1 Cor. 16:1), "the churches of Macedonia" (2 Cor. 8:1), and "the seven churches which are in Asia" (Rev. 1:4) support the traditional position of Baptists in this interpretation. To refer to "The Baptist Church" as one thinks of the denomination is incorrect. The word "church" as we use it, and as we believe the Bible teaches it, refers in most instances to an independent, local body. This idea seems strange to some religious groups. We must ever consider the individual congregation to be the primary and principle unit for carrying on the kingdom's work on earth. It needs, however, to be remembered that there are at least two instances where the word "church" is used in a broader sense (Matt. 16:18; Eph 5:23) and evidently refers to the world body of the redeemed. These exceptions do not remove the emphases of the New Testament on the church as a local congregation.

Church membership is reserved for people who meet certain specific requirements. Those who fail to qualify are never church members in the fullest meaning of the term. Names can be on rolls even when lives are lived apart from the church.

One does not logically qualify for membership in a Baptist church by meeting the membership requirements of some other denomination. It would be presumptuous for a person to assume or ask this. Would a Mason be justified in asking membership in the Elks Club on his Masonic initiation? Just as naturalization requirements are set up by the Federal Government and not by a foreigner applying for citizenship, so the Bible sets up the standards of church membership. Those requirements are not determined by the persons applying for church membership. The principle is just that simple. When a person requests a Baptist church to change or lower its church membership requirements in order that he might be received more easily into its membership, the church is made to wonder whether that candidate wants to join the church or whether he wants the church to join him. No church can lower the high divine standards for church membership on the insistence of men without compromise on an important Bible principle.

(2) Conversion, first requirement.—The very first requirement for church membership is the genuine experience of conversion on the part of the individual. Without that birth from above which brings salvation, one is not ready for membership in a New Testament church. The church is made up of baptized believers. One must be "born again" by God's grace before he can be acquainted with spiritual things. Until that personal and spiritual experience comes, he is not ready for baptism or church membership. An experience of conversion is the very first requirement. That fact constitutes one of the most important teachings of the Bible. We often refer to this requirement as the necessity for a regenerate membership. It simply means that the members must be converted before they are ready to become church members.

All through the Scriptures there are verses which let us know that conversion must precede baptism. (See Acts 2:38,41 and 2 Cor. 8:5.) Faith comes first. Baptism follows. They must come in that exact order or the symbol of baptism is meaningless.

(3) Unredeemed on church rolls.—Without a true conversion experience church membership becomes mere make-believe. Names can be on the church roll without their being written on God's book of life. For that reason churches must of necessity be very cautious in receiving new members. As far as is humanly possible, they must make sure of their previous conversion and sincere purposes.

People cannot pray with effectiveness when they are strangers to the God who answers prayer. Needless to say, some churches have been brought to grief and spiritual paralysis by having listed men and women on their rolls who have never truly trusted Christ. To baptize people before they have had an experience of personal salvation is to mislead them. It is also to disregard plain Bible teachings.

Christians are basically different. That fact must ever remain. Christ makes that difference. Any pastor has grounds for concern when there are those on the roll of the church who have never truly trusted Christ and who live like people on the outside of the church. He faces terrific and impossible problems of fellowship and instruction. Men cannot discern spiritual truth until conversion enables them to see the invisible things of God (John 3:3). They cannot learn much about Christ until they know Christ.

3. The Ordinances of the Church

The church in New Testament times had two ordinances. Baptists try to maintain both of them in simple purity. They are highly meaningful and exceedingly beautiful. Each is a symbol portraying spiritual truth. They symbolize. They picture a spiritual truth in a visible way. One ordinance portrays the change of the human heart through faith in Christ. The other pictures the Saviour in His work of sacrifice which purchased that salvation.

(1) Baptism.—The first ordinance is baptism. This ordinance in the New Testament days was always by immersion. It was administered always to those who already had believed. When people trusted Christ, they then submitted to baptism by immersion. The ordinance pictures in dramatic fashion the burial to an old life of sin and the resurrection of a new life in Christ (Rom. 6:4). It also declares faith in a Christ who died, was buried, and rose again. This specific biblical truth is not correctly portrayed unless the one who is being baptized has been converted first. Nor is the meaning rightfully given unless that candidate is baptized by immersion. To change the mode of baptism is to alter entirely the message and meaning of the ordinance.

The presence of baptistries in the ancient Catholic churches of Rome and the Anglican churches of England confirms historical data that those bodies in former times baptized by immersion.

Baptists rigidly hold to the ancient form of baptism by immersion for the sake of truth and right. In the light of Bible teaching we could not do otherwise. We adhere unfailingly to the New Testament pattern, believing that Jesus gave it in that form deliberately and with purpose.

Baptists do not believe that baptism is necessary to salvation. Water has no power to erase human sins. One is not saved by water. Nor is he saved by water and blood. "The blood of Jesus Christ His Son cleanseth us from all sin" (1 John 1:7). If blood cleanses from all sin, there is no sin remaining for the baptismal waters to wash away. If baptism had been so essential to soul cleansing, why would Jesus and Paul have failed to baptize (John 4:2; 1 Cor. 1:17)? Or how could the thief on the cross have been saved by his faith (Luke 23:43) when he never had opportunity to be baptized?

We Baptists do consider baptism essential to obedience, thought it is not necessary for soul cleansing. Jesus would not have walked so far and at great inconvenience to be baptized at the hands of John in the river Jordan had He not considered baptism significant. Baptism is a unique manner of confession of one's faith in Christ. It identifies him with Christ and His church.

Baptists consider baptism to be a church ordinance. The Great Commission ordering us to baptize believers was, as we see it, given to the early church. For that reason we seek church approval by vote of the membership authorizing the baptism of each candidate. That approval authorizes the minister to baptize the candidate on the profession of his faith in Christ. The church, therefore, expresses its belief that all New Testament requirements have been fully met. Freelance baptism, which is done apart from the church, is not New Testament baptism. That is true even if it is done by immersion.

The administrator of the ordinance of baptism must not only baptize believers by immersion on the authority of the church, but he must himself be a baptized believer in Christ. In addition, the baptism must be for the purpose of symbolizing a real spiritual conversion by the candidate. Such was invariably true in New Testament times.

(2) The Lord's Supper.—The other ordinance of the New Testament is the Lord's Supper. The Memorial Supper of our Lord was instituted by Christ during the closing week of His earthly ministry, on the night when He and His disciples were observing the Passover. It is really a portrayal of His crucified life.

Knowing our human frailty and tendency to forget, Jesus gave this meaningful picture of Himself. It shows how He wants most to be remembered. It is an ordinance which is to be observed periodically in remembrance of the fact that Jesus submitted to the supreme sacrifice of death that men might be saved. This ordinance portrays Jesus in His meaningful mission of human redemption.

The fruit of the vine symbolizes Jesus' shed blood. The bread portrays His surrendered body. Taken separately the bread and fruit of the vine picture the death of Christ on the cross for human sin. By the eating and drinking the fact is symbolized that the power of the crucified Christ reaches every area of human living to redeem it and become vital spiritual energy for daily Christian living. The Lord's Supper does not cleanse. It does symbolize the only power of cleansing known for the human soul.

There is no biblical requirement concerning the frequency with which the church is to observe the ordinance of the Lord's Supper. One might partake of it weekly, monthly, quarterly, or annually without violation of the commandment or spirit. The Bible simply says, "This do ye, as oft as ye drink it, in remembrance of me" (1 Cor. 11:25). More important than the frequency is the spirit in which the ordinance is observed.

Regarding qualifications for one's eligibility to partake of the Lord's Supper, there have been differences of interpretation. We as Baptists have been called "close communionists," meaning that we attempt to limit those who partake of the Lord's Supper to those who are members of our churches. If one faces the question fairly, however, he must admit that every denomination practices some form of "close communion." Not any church or denomination would throw open its doors to invite any and all people of all beliefs or no belief to partake of the Supper of the Lord. Such practice would be unthinkable. All denominations and all churches teach that those who partake must meet certain requirements, and rightly so. It is the Lord's Supper. Actually, Jesus is the one who did the limiting. We cannot be free to liberalize the teachings of Jesus at this point lest we offend Him and mar one of His wise purposes.

Baptists follow rigidly the teaching that baptism by immersion is a prerequisite for partaking of the Lord's Supper. As far as we can learn from the Scriptures, those who partook were always baptized believers. By logic the ordinances should come in just that order. Baptism must come first. The Lord's Supper should come second. The point of theological difference has come when we require baptism to be by immersion of a believer on church authority, by a proper administrator, and for the Scriptural purpose. What is usually labeled "close communion" is in reality "close baptism."

We cannot consistently hold that baptism by immersion is necessary to qualify for church membership and then change that mode of baptism to some other form when one seeks to qualify for partaking of the Lord's Supper. If baptism by immersion is necessary for church membership, the same mode of baptism is essential to qualify one scripturally to partake of the Lord's Supper.

In partaking of the Supper, there must never be a spirit of pride, self-righteousness, or hatred. The thought of all that Jesus did for us at Calvary should drive such earthly feelings from our lives. That is something of what Paul meant when he commanded that we partake of the Supper "worthily" (1 Cor. 11:27). We can never be worthy to partake of it. We can partake of it worthily.

4. The Democracy of the Church.

(1) All members have equal rights.—A Baptist church is one of the purest democracies in the world. All members have the same rights and privileges. Each one can enter into full discussion of all matters brought before the church for deliberation and decision.

The deacons are church officers (1 Tim. 3:8-13) but in no sense do they constitute a legislative body for the church. They are servants of the church, not lords over it. The deacons are selected by the church from the finest men of the membership. However, this does not grant them an unscriptural authority to control the church. They are to carry out the will of the church. Church decisions must be made by the church body as a whole.

The business meetings of the church, whether they are held monthly or quarterly, are for the purpose of determining issues and programs before the church. The pastor, who is also a church officer (1 Tim. 3:1-7), or some appointed moderator, presides. Matters are decided by a majority vote of the membership. While each member of the church can speak and vote, it is well that he keep in mind that he is a member of the body but that Christ is the head. It is the duty of the body to submit to the wishes of the Head. Christ's will must, therefore, be sought and followed.

This system of church government, a pure democracy, magnifies the worth of the individual member of the church. Everybody is somebody. Recognition is given to each individual. He is given a free voice and vote in all affairs of church government and life as he feels God's Spirit leading him.

(2) The priesthood of the believer.—The "priesthood of the believer" is a real belief and practice of Baptists. (See 1 Peter 2:5.) Approaches to God do not need to be made through the channel of human ministers or earthly priests. Each person has direct access to the Almighty through Christ. Therefore, each one has a right to express his feelings concerning the Lord's leading in his own life. God's leadership over a group is determined only as each person of that group expresses the deep feelings of his own heart. That is why the church votes on church matters. It is the only method of determining the leadership of God over a group of people. Each one interprets divine leadership in his own individual life and expresses that leadership through his vote in church meetings.

(3) Unionizing forces would compromise our beliefs.—Baptists generally are suspicious of unionizing agencies and organizations. At times we have suffered sharp attack because of our convictions and stand on the matter of local church independence. Baptists do not have an attitude of snobbishness, but of separateness. Our loyalty to the church and our own denomination is based on fidelity to New Testament teaching.

The position of Baptists on church union is not difficult to understand. Our emphasis is on the importance and individuality of the church. This emphasis has kept us from going into interdenominational groups along with many other denominations, national and international. Baptists have steered clear of interdenominationalism on one hand and nondenominationalism on the other. We have always sought to remain independent and self-governing. Even our own denominational associations and conventions have no authority over the churches. They can exercise only the jurisdiction which the churches choose to yield or assign to them. Convention officers are servants of churches and not masters over them.

Are Protestant denominations which are now seeking "a world church" admitting that Catholics have been right through the years? Are they not trying to build a world church for Protestants by a similar pattern of centralized church government which Catholics have used through the centuries? Certainly Baptists are not anxious to become affiliated with such an organization or movement.

We Baptists have had many sad experiences of persecution in our long years of glorious history. We have found ourselves standing alone on many occasions. It is to be expected of us that we maintain an independent position now though many other denominations are working for interdenominational alliances. It is our natural position and attitude. We prefer to remain ourselves. To yield authority to some outside agency, whether regional, national, or international, runs contrary to the traditional Baptist position and practice in church government and administration. Unionization is made even more impossible by the radical and liberal theological views of certain religious groups with which we would become aligned automatically if we participated in the unionizing movements. We would become organizationally associated with some who minimize the inspiration of the Bible, belittle the atonement of Christ, and reject the necessity for a personal experience of faith in Jesus. On these vital points of Bible doctrine we cannot yield or compromise. It would be tragic for our churches and denomination.

We as Baptists have developed a worldwide program of our own. We are seeking to carry out the Great Commission in the fullest possible way as an independent and responsible denomination.

God is blessing our efforts. Conscious of our universal duty, we are already active in worldwide missionary responsibilities. What more could be asked or expected?

Not for one moment do we as Baptists look upon other denominations and churches with derision or scorn. We look upon any believer in the Lord Jesus Christ with love and a fraternal spirit. We would defend to the end of time their right to worship God as they choose. That is consistent with our traditional Baptist position on religious freedom. We would grant to them the privileges we ask for ourselves. At the same time, we ask for ourselves the same privilege of worshiping God as independent Baptist bodies, unfettered by unionizing compromises, and unhampered by the regulating or restraining influences of church overlords or governmental heads.

5. The Fellowship of the Church

(1) Christian fellowship superlative.—Of all the meaningful fellowships in the world, the finest and best is that which Christians within the same church and denomination feel toward each other. It is not a mere surface emotion. It is a feeling as deep and rich as life itself. With members of our own church group we feel a depth of love and fellowship such as belongs to one big family. "We know that we have passed from death unto life, because we love the brethren" (1 John 3:14). Love for the brethren within the church is very real in the Christian's life. It is very meaningful as life's battles are fought and life's burdens are born.

(2) Strength through Christian fellowship.—The desire to attend the preaching services of the church is very real. A Christian wishes to hear the Word of God proclaimed in sermon and song. He delights wholeheartedly in fellowship with his fellow Christian worshippers.

During revival meeting in a southern city, the evangelist was making afternoon ministerial calls. He chanced to visit an elderly woman handicapped by deafness. Because of her extreme difficulty in hearing, she had not been able to attend the worship services in her own church for many years. Seeing that her radio at home was equipped with special earphones to help overcome her deafness, she was asked if she listened to sermons over the radio. She answered alertly: "Yes, I hear excellent sermons over the radio almost every day. They are good, but they don't quite satisfy. When the preacher gets through with his sermon, I can't get up and shake hands with the radio." Her deep desire was for Christian fellowship as well as worship and instruction. It is a natural and deep Christian yearning.

Christian fellowship does not limit itself merely to the worship services on Sunday. It does include all church services, of course. Many outside relationships are affected also by one's faith in Christ. "Let us do good unto all men, especially unto them who are of the household of faith" (Gal. 6:10). This verse suggests that in every area of life the Christian spirit is to prevail. Christian fellowship is an endless relationship. All human relationships are to be motivated by the love of God within the Christian's heart for his brethren. This feeling of love is provided by God. It is God guided. How it does enrich human living!

(3) Foretaste of fellowship in heaven.– The delights of Christian fellowship here on earth provide a foretaste of the wondrous joys of that eternal fellowship in heaven. We are strengthened and helped by the company of the redeemed here and now. In heaven we shall have endless fellowship with the saints of the ages past and present. We shall live in the presence of the disciples and believers through the centuries. We shall also experience reunion with the loved ones and relatives who in faith and yet by death have gone on to be with God. Best of all, we will be with Jesus (John 14:3) in His unending presence and rewarding fellowship. Each member has his part to contribute of the spirit and life of the church. Some churches are cordial and warm because their members are that way. Other congregations are looked upon as formal and cold. The attitude of the individual member makes a difference in the spirit and attitude of the whole church. If each member contributes his rightful part to the warmth and fellowship of the church services, that church will be noted for its hospitality, cordiality, and spirituality.

Knowing that the church is a divine institution with a holy mission and a high purpose, we will give it our sacrificial best. It stands for truth, love, and fellowship. It furthers the message of hope and comfort. It provides a means of service and a circle of close friends with whom to labor. Such an institution stands high in God's purpose and plan. It has many competitors. It has no equals.

Membership in the church means much to our daily lives. We shall make the most of church membership for Jesus' sake as well as for our own happiness.

SUMMARY OF CHAPTER 2
THE MEANING OF CHURCH MEMBERSHIP

Introduction

1. The Church a Divine Institution
  (1) Jesus established the church (Matt. 16:18a)
  (2) The Great Commission given to the church (Matt. 28:19-20)
  (3) Victory promised the church (Matt. 16:18b)

2. The Membership of the Church
  (1) The New Testament meaning of the church (Rev. 1:4)
  (2) Conversion, first requirement (Acts 2:41)
  (3) Unredeemed on church rolls (1 John 2:19)

3. The Ordinances of the Church
  (1) Baptism (Rom. 6:4)
  (2) The Lord's Supper (1 Cor. 11:25)

4. The Democracy of the Church
  (1) All members have equal rights (1 Cor. 12:14-27)
  (2) The priesthood of the believer (1 Peter 2:5)
  (3) Unionizing forces would compromise our beliefs (2 Tim. 3:5)

5. The Fellowship of the Church
  (1) Christian fellowship superlative (1 John 3:14)
  (2) Strength through Christian fellowship (Matt. 18:20)
  (3) Foretaste of fellowship in heaven (John 14:3)

QUESTIONS FOR DISCUSSION
CHAPTER 2

1. Who established the church? When? Why?
2. Discuss the qualifications for church membership.
3. Name the ordinances of the church and tell their meaning.
4. Why do Southern Baptists avoid church union?
5. Describe the value of church fellowship.

COMMITMENT
For the New Church Member

Knowing that the church is a divine institution with a holy mission, I hereby commit myself in deepest loyalty to its doctrines, purposes, and program. I will give myself in devotion to the church because of my love for Christ, its Founder and Head.

(Signed) _____

Chapter 3

Your Life & Your Church

YOU AND YOUR CHURCH

The church belongs to Christ. We refer to it here as your church. We are not suggesting possession but relationship. It is your church in a similar sense in which America is your country.

Your church likely did many things for you before you became one of its members. As a child you doubtless attended its services, thrilled at the Bible lessons, sang with its members, and loved its pastor. At that time Christ was to you a historical character instead of personal Saviour. You were not ready then for church membership. After you accepted Christ as your own personal Saviour, you were baptized into the membership of the church. You became a member in full fellowship to enjoy all the privileges of its life and help. You found that the church was in a position then to mean more than ever before.

You should thank God that your church did not consider its obligation to you ended when you were won to Christ. Even a greater opportunity began for your church and you the moment you accepted Jesus as your Saviour. When you were converted, the church assumed the responsibility of giving you a lifetime of spiritual nurture, guidance, and instruction. It is your church's responsibility and task to help you grow into a strong and vigorous Christian.

At whatever age a person might accept Christ, he begins his Christian life as a spiritual infant. His church must accept the responsibility of nurturing and guiding him in spiritual growth if he is to become a strong and mature servant of God.

Your church can do many things for you to help you grow spiritually.

1. What Your Church Can Do for You

(1) It can help you in your worship life.—The ability to worship is limited to mankind. Let us illustrate. A boy owns a dog. That dog is in some ways the boy's superior. It can run faster, swim better, and perhaps eat more. But when the boys kneels to pray, that boy is in a realm his pet cannot enter. Only human beings can commune with God.

Worship is very necessary in human growth and happiness. Worship is soul nurture. It is fellowship with God. It is the expression of one's adoration for the Almighty. Worship is to the soul what food is to the body. It must not be neglected. The soul like the body can suffer malnutrition. To refuse to eat is to dwarf one's body. To refuse to worship is to halt or arrest one's spiritual development.

Your church seeks to direct your worship in the right way in order that you might live close to God. Worship in the church is necessary to vital Christian living. A man can worship God in private, but he finds that group worship is essential also. "Not forsaking the assembling of ourselves together, as the manner of some is" (Heb. 10:25) is God's statement of desire concerning our church attendance. A man can pray in public. It is significant, however, that those who attend church and participate in group worship are the selfsame ones who pray most at home. Public worship, family altars, and private devotions are guided by your church. You are encouraged to participate in them with sincerity and regularity.

Worship services are held for the benefit of the worshipers as well as the glory of God. The worshiper is encouraged to give something of himself, his talents, and energies, in the praise and service of God. True worship must be active. Participation is necessary. The one who engages in worship through singing, giving, and serving is the one who goes away with the greatest blessings.

(2) It can teach you the Word of God.—The task of teaching has been given to the church. The church is commanded to continue its task

of teaching until all Christians are fully practicing the things which Jesus taught and preached.

A church which feels its responsibility to each individual and discharges its duty well is thrilled to see the spiritual development in its members. Conversion is in reality the beginning of Christian experience. It is certainly not the end.

The Sunday School is a tremendously effective force in Bible teaching. It is actually the church fulfilling the command of Christ to teach the Word. Your church has selected and elected Sunday School teachers and officers with caution. They are great Christians whose faith and lives honor Christ. On each Sunday morning they lead their classes to delve deeply into the wonderful spiritual truths of God's Word. The study is not only a real joy, but a great spiritual benefit. Many of life's most serious questions find their answers through Bible study in the Sunday School class.

The lessons which are taught in Sunday School are directly from the Word of God. The Bible is the textbook. All other materials are helps in clarification and interpretation. God's truths are interpreted in the light of modern-day needs. They help Christians to grow in real spiritual strength. The Sunday School is the greatest force in mass Bible teaching in the world today.

The Sunday School is a mighty force in teaching and interpreting the Word of God. It is a source of tremendous influence as people join their hearts and hands in the effort to reach the masses for systematic Bible study.

(3) It can train you in church membership.—The church also gives supervised training. This, too, is fundamental. Mental knowledge alone is insufficient. One can know in his mind how an automobile should be driven. This fact does not necessarily qualify him for a driver's license. Someone can memorize a cookbook without being able to prepare a single meal.

The Discipleship Training program is for the purpose of giving guided growth and development. It is a marvelous way in which one can learn how to do the work of the Christian through the life of the church.

As practice is valuable to the athlete, the Discipleship Training program is important to the Christian. A church member must never think he has fully developed his skills and no longer needs training. When a Christian quits being a learner, he ceases to grow. His ability to serve diminishes proportionately. The Discipleship Training program is not for young people only, but for Christians of all ages. A person is never too young to learn. He is never too old to gain additional knowledge and inspiration. Learning and growing must of necessity continue throughout one's life. That is why the Discipleship Training program is for all ages.

It is impossible to estimate the number of people in church leadership today who received their basic guidance for Christian service in this program. It is in the Discipleship Training program that one learns to speak in public, pray before groups, preside over assemblies, and work with others in a cooperative way. The Discipleship Training program is the church preparing its members for efficient church membership.

(4) It can enlarge your missionary vision.—The Woman's Missionary Union and Baptist Men on Mission have definite and distinctive functions. They are organizations of the church which share missionary information and inspire missionary zeal.

The Woman's Missionary Union is composed of Women on Mission, Acteens, Girls in Action, Royal Ambassadors, and Mission Friends. The Woman's Missionary Union seeks to enlist these groups in a systematic study of the missionary teachings of the Bible and the missionary program of the denomination.

General headquarters for Woman's Missionary Union is in Birmingham, Alabama. State offices are also located in all of the states of the Southern Baptist Convention to keep the services close to the people.

Baptist Men on Mission is the name given to the organization for men who are mobilized for the support of the total program of the church. It seeks to carry on local missionary and church projects which enlist men in missions, evangelism, and general church work. Baptist Men on Mission is part of the North American Mission Board located in Alpharetta, Georgia. It has capable and consecrated leaders in each of the various states of the Southern Baptist Convention to help promote this work.

(5) It can assign you definite tasks to perform.—Your church seeks to give a specific assignment to every member every Sunday. This makes the church a mighty mobilized army. Each person has a specific job to do. This principle is vital in the life of the church and the Christian. Life stagnates without activity. Each person should have a Christian work to do during the week, and every person should be expected to be present for the worship service on every Sunday. To attend Sunday School and Discipleship Training as well as the worship services should be considered necessary in the life of each Christian on every Lord's Day.

The tasks within the church are many and varied. Members can teach, lead groups in training, sing or lead in singing, and witness to the lost in many ways. They can give. They can pray. Some members are capable of making posters, others of writing articles for newspaper publicity. Some can keep records skillfully, can make visits while others can plan programs or direct social activities in ways that will honor Christ. Some can be church librarians, others can handle audiovisual materials for the purpose of illustrating spiritual truth in a dramatic and visible way. There is a person in each church to do every job that needs to be done. It is not an easy thing to discover that leadership. It is harder still to organize the forces so that each person is in the particular place in which his services are best suited and where he finds maximum happiness. That ultimate end result must be the effort of the church. Leaders must be discovered and trained constantly.

After all is said and done, people do not grow spiritually in the same manner in which the proverbial farmer's goose is fattened. Its feet were nailed to the floor while its craw was stuffed. Christians are more like athletes in their spiritual growth. They strengthen through exercise, as well as food and directed activity. The more intense the activity, the finer the training. Church leaders should never fear overworking the church members. Those who work the hardest are the ones who grow the fastest. They are also the ones who are the happiest in the Lord.

2. What You Can Do Through Your Church

(1) You can cooperate with other Baptists in work and fellowship.— Cooperation in the church is a necessity. Team play can accomplish what individual action will never produce.

As Christians are bound together in closely knit church activity, they can have a tremendous influence over any community. Because of this power in united effort within the church, the devil attempts to destroy that unity. He would like to replace church fellowship with strife. He endeavors to produce factions and pressure groups which would rob the church of unity and power.

The unity and the cooperation of Baptist churches amaze the world. What holds Baptists together? There is no ecclesiastical head to issue orders or keep members and churches "in line." Fortunately, ours is a unity based on mutual faith in Christ rather than on union formulated in superficial fashion at a man-made level.

Just as each part of the human body has a specific function and yet each part must work in the interest of the whole body (read 1 Cor. 12:14-31), so each person and each church, while independent in function and purpose, must work together voluntarily for the common good. Without united effort we have only guerrilla warfare. By intensified action, as we follow our great Commander, we meet Satan's forces with a blitzkrieg. Guerrilla warfare may disturb an enemy. It is the blitzkrieg which utterly defeats an enemy.

Baptists work together on the voluntary principle of cooperation in associations, state conventions, the Southern Baptist Convention, and the Baptist World Alliance.

The *associations* are made up of churches of a small geographical area, usually covering a county. The *state conventions* conform almost identically to state lines. The Southern Baptist Convention is made up of more than half of the states in the United States. The constitution of the *Southern Baptist Convention*, however, provides for it to exist or function anywhere in the territorial United States or its possessions when certain other qualifications are met. The *Baptist World Alliance* is a worldwide fellowship of Baptist churches covering the nations of the earth.

Baptists are better learning the fine art of working together harmoniously. This is increasing both their efficiency and effectiveness. The rapid progress of their growth and cooperation the world over is encouraging and thrilling.

(2) You can give that God's work may grow.—Giving is God's plan. It is not man's scheme for raising money, but God's plan for saving men from covetousness by building in them a spirit of Christian generosity. Not only does the one who receives the gift get a blessing but the giver is benefited as well. Gifts made through our churches are carefully handled and prayerfully used in the best manner determined by those churches. Each contribution is made with a prayer that the gift shall honor the Lord. In a later chapter full discussion is made of the scriptural program of giving through the church. At this point we only call attention to the fact that the church does provide a Christian the means through which his contribution can be made to bless the world. The Baptist plan of giving is through the church.

(3) You can best serve God through your church.—Many ways are afforded the Christian to serve Christ. The best way is through his church. As he serves Christ in that relationship, he is identifying himself with the most important organization and work on earth. He is working with others who can inspire, help, and encourage him. Christ was wonderfully wise in providing us churches in which to work and grow.

3. The Covenant of the Church

Baptists have no church officers to determine what they are to be, do, believe, or teach. The Bible stands as the final authority for Baptists in all matters of faith and practice. It is used as the basis for all church ordinances, requirements for membership, doctrines, and beliefs. Neither the church nor the denomination claims that it has the right to alter or revise Bible revelation and commandments. The church's task is to proclaim, not alter God's Word.

(1) What a covenant is.—Our Baptist churches, while they do not have creeds, do have covenants. There is quite a difference. These covenants draw together the mutual thoughts and purposes of the members. They express the most outstanding beliefs and

resolutions of their hearts. They state the hopes, desires, ambitions, and pledges of church members who have come together to serve the Lord. These covenants express the whole-hearted intentions of these Christians to pray and labor diligently and unitedly for the advancement of Christ's kingdom and the meeting of spiritual objectives for Him.

(2) A sample covenant.—The church covenant used by many churches, and distributed widely by LifeWay Christian Resources reads:

"Having been led, as we believe by the Spirit of God, to receive the Lord Jesus Christ as our Savior and, on the profession of our faith, having been baptized in the name of the Father, and of the Son, and of the Holy Spirit, we do now, in the presence of God, and this assembly, most solemnly and joyfully enter into covenant with one another, as one body in Christ.

"We engage, therefore, by the aid of the Holy Spirit to walk together in Christian love; to strive for the advancement of this church, in knowledge, holiness, and comfort; to promote its prosperity and spirituality; to sustain its worship, ordinances, discipline, and doctrines; to contribute cheerfully and regularly to the support of the ministry, the expenses of the church, the relief of the poor, and the spread of the gospel through all nations.

"We also engage to maintain family and secret devotions; to religiously educate our children; to seek the salvation of our kindred and acquaintances; to walk circumspectly in the world; to be just in our dealings, faithful in our engagements, and exemplary in our deportment; to avoid all tattling, backbiting, and excessive anger; to abstain from the sale of, and use of destructive drugs or intoxicating drinks as a beverage; to shun pornography; to be zealous in our efforts to advance the Kingdom of our Savior.

"We further engage to watch over one another in brotherly love; to remember one another in prayer; to aid one another in sickness and distress; to cultivate Christian sympathy in feeling and Christian courtesy in speech; to be slow to take offense, but always ready for reconciliation and mindful of the rules of our Savior, to secure it without delay.

"We moreover engage that when we remove from this place we will, as soon as possible, unite with some other church where we can carry out the spirit of this covenant and the principles of God's Word."

(3) Living up to the covenant.—It is good to have the church members read the church covenant in unison periodically. Many churches do this once each quarter. Some churches read the covenant on the days on which the Lord's Supper is observed. While this is optional, it proves to be very profitable. The important thing is for Christians to be true to their vows to God and to one another by conscientiously living up to the pledges set forth in the covenant.

The church is very important in its contribution to the lives of Christians. No child of God should try to serve Christ very long without seeking church membership. A Christian outside of the church is somewhat like an orphan. He may grow into manhood, but the hardship of doing so without parental guidance will make that growth harder, if not stunted. The desire of the Christian is to grow to healthy spiritual maturity through the church and its organizations. That is the way Jesus planned it for us.

SUMMARY OF CHAPTER 3
YOU AND YOUR CHURCH

Introduction

1. *What Your Church Can Do for You*
   (1) It can help you in your worship life (John 4:23-24)
   (2) It can teach you the Word of God (Psalm 119:130)
   (3) It can train you in church membership (1 Cor. 1:4-8)
   (4) It can enlarge your missionary vision (John 4:35)
   (5) It can assign you definite tasks to perform (Rom. 12:4-8)

2. *What You Can Do Through Your Church*
   (1) You can cooperate with other Baptists in work and fellowship (1 Cor. 3:9)
   (2) You can give that God's work may grow (1 Cor. 16:2)
   (3) You can best serve God through your church (Heb. 10:25)

3. *The Covenant of the Church*
   (1) What a covenant is (1 Peter 3:15)
   (2) A sample covenant
   (3) Living up to the covenant (Acts 18:18)

QUESTIONS FOR DISCUSSION

Chapter 3

1. Discuss the value of worship in a Christian life.
2. Describe the work of the Sunday School and tell its relation to the church.
3. Tell how the Discipleship Training program can help you develop into a happier and stronger Christian.
4. How can the church help you enlarge your missionary interest and vision?
5. Name some Christian services you can render through your church.

COMMITMENT

For the New Church Member

Believing that my life will be infinitely richer in spiritual things if I am loyal to the church of the Lord Jesus Christ, I pledge myself to be faithful to its teaching, prayerful in my attitude toward it, and cooperative with its members as we labor together for the world's salvation and Christ's glory.

(Signed) _____

Chapter 4

Your Life & Your Church

YOUR STEWARDSHIP

A steward is a keeper. He is not an owner. He handles that which rightfully belongs to another. He feels accountable personally for the careful protection and wise use of that which is entrusted to him. He handles the possession of the owner with more caution and concern than he would if it were his very own.

As Christians we are not owners of earthly things. We are users and keepers of God's possessions. We must care for and use God's possessions as the great Owner desires.

A Christian feels obligated to carry on God's business with personal dedication. He is devoted to the task of handling aright the things which God has lent him to hold and use. Someday each person will be rewarded for his faithfulness or called to give a reason for his negligence. That makes it important that we be the right kind of stewards now.

You as a Christian must personally face the matter of stewardship and decide right now what attitudes and actions will be yours as you handle possessions for God. Handling His affairs aright is very important. The principle of stewardship, if practiced aright, must first be understood and appreciated.

1. What the Bible Teaches About Stewardship

It is not left to the Christian to formulate his own ideas about Christian giving. The Bible instructs us in detail. God is specific in His teachings about man's obligations in the handling of God's business.

(1) The earth belongs to God.—"The earth is the Lord's and the fullness thereof; the world, and they that dwell therein" (Psalm 24:1). There must never be a question mark in the mind of any Christian about the ownership or management of the world. The Bible tells us that the human race, while inhabiting the earth, does not own it. It is God's without question. The Bible is very clear on that point.

The earth is God's by right of creation. No one argues the claim of an author to a manuscript. An automobile manufacturer legally controls the cars he has made. By the same principle the Bible says that the world belongs to God. "God created the heaven and the earth" (Gen. 1:1). This verse recognizes God as the rightful owner because of that first creative act.

The earth is the Lord's by right of supervision. He cares for the earth which He has made. He has never abandoned it for one moment. God has always ruled over the world. Men who see aright will declare with David that the whole earth declares the handiwork of God. They will recognize that only a God of true greatness could shape a world so vast and magnificent. If one views the wonders of the world through correct eyes, he will see the might of God's hand everywhere. He will see God in the beauty of each flower, the mysterious migration of birds, and the amazing laws of nature. The marvels of creation prove God's wisdom and power.

(2) Christians belong to God.—"Know ye not that . . . ye are not your own? Ye are bought with a price" (1 Cor. 6:19-20).

We ourselves were made by God. Man is the crowning product of God's creative act. God made man in His own image. He gave him the power to love, the right to choose, and the ability to think. He gave to man a soul which is immortal. He made him like Himself because He wanted him for Himself. The very creative act, so glorious and complete, declares that man also belongs to God.

We are God's by right of redemption. He not only made us, but He bought us back. Great was the price He paid. The cross of Calvary expresses the depth to which God was willing to reach to purchase man's soul freedom and redemption. It is hard for us to understand the price which God paid for human salvation. We know that Jesus paid a tremendous price by His sacrificial death on the cross. But how much did human salvation cost God? A Christian father expressed God's part this way: "Knowing as I do the curse of sin and the lost condition of men, I think I could bring myself to the point of dying if by my death sinners could be saved. I could give my own life. But to give my own son—never." When we remember that God gave His Son, we can measure in a fragmentary way what His sensitive heart must have suffered as He witnessed the agonies of His Son on the cross. God was willing to pay the awful price because of His love for man (Isa. 53:10). Truly the price He paid also makes us belong wholly to Him.

(3) You must give an account of your faithfulness in stewardship (see Luke 13:6-9 and Matt. 25:14-30).—Oftentimes human records are carelessly kept. God's records are complete, and without flaw. In the light of God's knowledge we will be measured and rewarded. Knowing that God is keeping constant check, it is well that we write the record that will please Him and bring us blessings. Opportunity to make our records correct is provided now. That chance will never come again. (See Matt. 25:1-13.) When life is gone, it is too late to roll back the years to start anew and write better life records. This sobering thought challenges the young and growing Christians to do their utmost from the start. It is the high road to happiness. God knows your faithfulness in stewardship. He will reward you accordingly.

2. The Stewardship of Your Life

Many think of stewardship in terms of dollars only. While material things enter into the picture, they cover only a small part of the whole Christian principle. Stewardship is as big as life itself. It actually enters into every area of human living. Your whole life belongs to God. That is the way you want to think of the stewardship of life as you plan and give your services in His name. Hands are to serve, feet are to go, the lips are to speak. Even the mind is to think the great thoughts of God.

(1) Hours for God's work.—When it comes to the measuring of time, we are all on the same footing. Each day has 24 hours, no more or no less. Every individual has the same amount of time in

each month and every year. The difference comes in the way we use that time. Each person organizes his day to do what he wants most to do. It is the Christian's obligation to so schedule his day and week that he can attend to the matters of God and his church in the right way. This should be considered a necessity in a Christian's planning of his calendar. The evil world would cross out the good from our days if we would only let it do so. It is the Christian's task to arrange his day so that a part can be scheduled for Christ's work. He must protect that time diligently so that God may have it for His work as He chooses.

(2) Abilities for God's use.—All men have talents. These talents differ as much as human faces or as leaves on a tree. Yet, there is no man without some talent. In the average church there are people who can do any kind of work. Some sing with skill, others usher with grace. Many can teach with effectiveness. Whatsoever your talent is, God has given it to you for use. To hide that talent is to make life a failure. To be timid and refuse to use it will rob you of growth and blessing. Dedicated talents in the lives of consecrated Christians can change the world.

(3) Influence for God's glory.—A Christian's influence is invisible to the human eye. Yet it is as real as the ocean. No man lives without influencing others. Some people influence the world badly. Other influence it for good. All people influence it. By your mode of living, manner of speech, honesty in dealing with others, and even by church attendance you are wielding an unconscious influence on the lives of others. As the shade of a tree reaches where that tree can never go, so the good influence of a godly life stretches out into a territory where your body can never go. When such is true, the life can reach forth into other lands, and extend even into other generations. Using all of life's talents for God is the demonstration of stewardship at its best.

3. Giving Starts with the Tithe

Before tithing was ever required in the Bible, it was put into practice by men. Study Genesis 14:18-20 and note that Abraham paid tithes to Melchizedek, king of Salem, priest of the Most High. It was practiced before the law of God ever demanded it. Abraham tithed because gratitude required it. His heart was so happy over the knowledge of what God had done in giving him victory in battle that he acknowledged God as the source of every blessing by tithing the tithe.

(1) The plan of the tithe.—God's plan is that every Christian make a gift every Sunday, that the gift be in proportion to his income, and that it be given in a spirit of gladness. God's Word sets forth those requirements in specific fashion. "Upon the first day of the week let every one of you lay by him in store, as God hath prospered him" (1 Cor. 16:2) illustrates this principle. "Not grudgingly, or of necessity: for God loveth a cheerful giver" (2 Cor. 9:7) adds the finishing touch to the full truth. These simple statements sum up the Bible's plan of the tithe with the four basic principles involved.

(2) The purpose of the tithe.—One purpose of the tithe is to bless the giver. "It is more blessed to give than to receive" (Acts 20:35). The giver in truth becomes a worldwide citizen as he actively engages in the worldwide missionary program of his church. Giving enlarges vision. When a portion of your gift goes to South America in missionary work, that land becomes closer to you than ever. It is no longer missions in a foreign land. It is something nearby and personal. The giver is blessed through the gift he gives. Giving according to God's plan saves the giver from greed and covetousness. It builds in him a spirit of concern and generosity.

The purpose of the tithe is also to bring good into the world. When a businessman makes financial investments, he sincerely hopes that he is rendering a service as well as making an income. Spiritual investments produce the longest returns. The tithe is a weekly investment in the spiritual welfare of the world. It is your personal donation to the mobilized effort of Christians to help halt the progress of infidelity and sin. It is given to foster the causes of Christ and to halt the world's decay. The task is so big that the united efforts and gifts of Christ's people who are numbered in the millions are required to meet the emergency. A little stream of income is not sufficient. It will take a might river. "The field is the world" (Matt. 13:38). Large and many must be the gifts, for huge is the task.

(3) The plea for the tithe.—While tithing is not to be engaged in by law in the strict Old Testament sense, it is to be remembered that

Jesus expressed His approval of it (Matt. 23:23). That very fact should make it obligatory in our lives. Jesus' expressed wish should be looked upon as binding on the Christian. Tithing, like love, is a natural expression of the Christian's attitude and experience.

Any Christian who sees the needs of the world wants to give. He cannot listen to the cries of orphan children for food and clothing and remain unconcerned. A Christian's heart is tender. If Christians do not hear the world's cries and care for its needs, who will? Hard-hearted men are not apt to do much about the situation.

The needs of mission fields are numerous and acute. Missionaries need to be sent. Sick people by the thousands await the healing touch of skilled hands. Young preachers need to be educated. The aged and infirmed must not be forgotten. Needs are everywhere. Christians are to tithe that their contributions through their churches might meet those needs by building orphanages and hospitals. The contributions will help send missionaries and helpers to care for needs of every kind, both material and spiritual. The Christian's heart is one of compassion and concern. He cannot listen to heart-rending pleas and see the tears of a needy world without doing something to help.

Happiness awaits you as a Christian when you are faithful in giving. No one has quite as many surprises awaiting him as the young Christian who dares to begin tithing early with seriousness and regularity. You will be amazed at the amount of money you can give. You will be astounded by the fact that nine-tenths of your salary will purchase more than the ten-tenths would formerly buy for you. You will be surprised at yourself for not having begun tithing earlier. You will be amazed that you had never before systematically measured the material blessings of God in your own life. You will find it almost unbelievable that God has done so much to enrich and bless you.

The young Christian who launches out on faith and begins to tithe finds heaven's doors opened and blessings from heaven in abundance coming his way. The promise of God remains in force. He will "open you the windows of heaven, and pour you out a blessing, that there shall not be room enough to receive it" (Mal. 3:10). God will not forget His word.

4. The Cooperative Program and Your Stewardship

The earth is big. The God of might made it. Billions of people live upon its surface. It is the plan of God that the full gospel shall be preached to all the people of the whole world. Life is so brief and Christian experience so individual that every generation brings hosts of lost souls on the horizon. It is a stupendous and endless task generation after generation to win multitudes of people to salvation.

How can this world ever be won? One man cannot do it. Nor can one congregation or one generation. The purpose of God, however, is plain. In His will the job can be done. Jesus instituted the churches over the land and ordered them to lead in the mighty missionary endeavor. God worked out a plan which linked together the lives of individuals and churches for this stupendous assignment whereby they might accomplish this task successfully. It is done without violating their individuality or losing sight of their local obligation and opportunities. The New Testament churches were interested in each other (2 Cor. 8:16-22). They sought to serve each other's welfare, and prayed for God to get the glory. So must we.

From earliest days the principle of mutual interest and voluntary cooperation among churches of like faith and order began to emerge. That principle has continued and has developed into our present denominational endeavors.

(1) Definition of the term.—The Cooperative Program in Southern Baptist terminology applies to the principle they fulfill the many binding missionary and benevolent obligations placed on them by the Bible. It is a method of church and missionary financing which is wholly voluntary. It is a program rather than a campaign. Cooperative Program is a name given to the agreed plan for missionary financing. It describes the plan whereby every Baptist can give each Sunday with one contribution to every cause supported by Baptists in the whole world. It is done by the placing of an undesignated gift in the offering plate of the church.

(2) Description of the plan.—The person who said, "I've been giving to the Cooperative Program for years, but when are we going to get that thing paid for?" woefully misunderstood the facts. Baptists do

not give to the Cooperative Program. They give through it. It is a channel through which contributions are made to the worthy causes which must be supported by a New Testament church. It will continue as long as those missionary causes are our Christian obligation. That means until Jesus comes again. The function is simple. It calls for the individual's gifts to be given regularly. Usually the gift is made in an offering envelope provided by the church so that accurate church records can be kept for the benefit of both the giver and the church. The church decides in advance just how the total undesignated contributions of the members shall be divided fairly among all causes. A part of each contribution remains in the church treasury to care for such local needs as building equipment, utilities, pastor's salary, and so on. An agreed percentage or amount is sent monthly to support causes outside of the church.

The ideal is for a church to divide each undesignated dollar contributed on a 50-50 basis. This means that fifty cents out of each dollar contributed goes for local needs and 50 cents to missionary and benevolent causes beyond the local field. The amount or percentage which each church will use in its own program is first determined. In the ideal church budget it would be 50 cents in each dollar. The remainder is designated for the Cooperative Program. The Cooperative amount is sent to the Baptist headquarters of the state to be proportionately divided once more between statewide and worldwide causes.

The state convention, after due deliberation and following a careful survey of needs, determines in advance what percentage of the amount sent to the state office will be used within the state in its own program of state missions. Baptist colleges, hospitals, orphanages, and many other similar causes are supported by the state convention out of the state's share of Cooperative Program receipts. Again the ideal is for each dollar to be divided on a fifty-fifty basis between the state convention and Southern Baptist Convention causes.

Convention-wide and worldwide causes are supported by the amount sent from the states for those additional missionary purposes through the Cooperative Program. The money is forwarded to the treasurer of the Executive Committee of the Southern Baptist Convention at 901 Commerce Street, Suite 750,

Nashville, Tennessee 37203. The Southern Baptist Convention previously determines the percentage of division among seminaries, national and international missions, and other causes fostered at the Convention-wide level of denominational organization. It is a simple but workable plan which is highly satisfactory to Southern Baptists.

The individual who desires to designate his gift to some special cause does so by writing instructions on the offering envelope stating the cause to which he wishes his offering to go. Through the Cooperative Program plan that individual would give an undesignated gift through a church envelope. Then, through his voice and vote in the church business meeting, he would help determine the percentages of division of the entire amount which he and all other church members give. In the latter plan, the proportions are determined before the contributions are made. The latter plan has generally proved to be the best and most satisfactory.

(3) Deepening appreciation.—In carrying out the above-described plan of giving, every cause which we as Baptists are obligated to support in our assignment of preaching, teaching, and healing is cared for with utmost economy, fairness, efficiency, and ease. If the divisions are made in the churches and within the states on the 50-50 basis, which is the ideal, then each undesignated dollar will be divided as follows: Fifty cents will be kept out of each dollar for work within the church; 25 cents will be used for missionary work in the state; the other 25 cents will go for Baptist work outside the state. The last share reaches out to the uttermost parts of the earth in vast and extensive missionary endeavors.

Baptist acceptance and support of the Cooperative Program has been phenomenal. It is ever deepening in its usefulness. Each year it is more efficiently and economically administered by the wisest and most consecrated men available to the Convention. Millions of dollars flow each month through thousands of church treasuries into state Baptist convention treasuries. From those states a proportion of the money is sent to Convention-wide and worldwide causes. As the Cooperative Program continues to strengthen and expand, our entire missionary force will be enlarged and extended. While the percentages of division might change slightly from year to year on the basis of adequacy or need, the principle remains the same. The movement rolls on unendingly. It has proved to be the most consistent and economical method for carrying forth in a financial way the affairs of the kingdom.

5. Your Church and Your Stewardship

(1) A worthy budget for missions and local expenses.—Most of our churches operate on the basis of a unified budget. This simply means that the undesignated contributions of the church members go into the general treasury of the church. Out of that treasury all the causes and interests of the church are financed. If the church approves its budget and sets its program at a challenging pace, much more will be accomplished than by any hit-or-miss method which is inevitable if the church has no budget or several budgets.

The unified budget helps free a church from the careless handling of church finances. It puts church business on a sound and efficient basis. No business in any community or city should be run with more efficiency than the church. To adopt the unified budget plan is to follow the proven system which has strengthened many churches. In that budget all causes and departments of church life are cared for adequately. The budget should be skillfully drawn and carefully adopted by the church. That budget should be followed carefully and rigidly as the year progresses.

(2) An enlistment program to reach each new member.—The church is to train its members in giving just as in praying, witnessing, and Bible study. Usually the church makes a visit to every church member individually sometime in the fall of each year to try to enlist that member in a program of regular giving during the approaching year. It is a part of the training program of the church. This special effort of personally enlisting church members in regular giving is an annual effort to enlist each member in the whole program of the church through regular week-by-week giving.

(3) Increase percentage of budget for Cooperative Program.— Some churches give specifically designated amounts in dollars through the Cooperative Program each year. Other churches prefer to give a percentage of the total contributions. The latter has proved best both for the churches and the causes fostered by them. On the basis of percentage, however, it is seen that some churches give woefully

little when the figures are finally tabulated. Churches should strive to give more to missions each succeeding year until at least 50 per cent is going to outside causes.

The ever-enlarging army of tithers among Southern Baptists is encouraging. How wonderful it is. Yet the amazing thing is that there are some who have not yet seen the vision or claimed the privilege.

It would be a happy day indeed if every Baptist tithed! The results would be phenomenal. The missionary forces could be enlarged and extended. Our Baptist colleges and seminaries could more adequately care for the multitudes of young men and women who wish to prepare for Christian leadership. In preaching, teaching, and healing, the efforts of our churches would be multiplied many times over.

Tithers grow through tithing. A young boy had just accepted Christ when he was invited to begin tithing. He began the first Sunday after his conversion by placing a nickel each week in the offering plate of the church. The small contribution meant little to the financial life of that church. What it has meant to the life of that boy has been beyond comprehension. As a new and young Christian he caught a vision of something big. He delighted in the privilege of participation in a worldwide Christian program of missions. It set for him the course of thinking and giving through years to come. It is to the definite interest of the Christian and the church that every Baptist be enlisted as a tither.

God's plan of giving is wise. It is sound and workable. Individuals or churches cannot improve on it. As it is learned and practiced by new Christians it will mean much to them. It will hasten the spread of God's truth over the whole earth. It will help young Christians grow in missionary passion and vision.

Will you begin to practice God's plan of giving now?

SUMMARY OF CHAPTER 4
YOUR STEWARDSHIP

Introduction

1. *What the Bible Teaches About Stewardship*
    (1) The earth belongs to God (Psalm 24:1)
    (2) Christians belong to God (1 Cor. 6:19-20)
    (3) You must give an account of your faithfulness in stewardship (Matt. 25:19)

2. *The Stewardship of Your Life*
    (1) Hours for God's work (Eph. 5:16)
    (2) Abilities for God's use (2 Tim. 1:6)
    (3) Influence for God's glory (Acts 4:13)

3. *Giving Starts with the Tithe*
    (1) The plan of the tithe (Matt. 23:23; 1 Cor. 16:2)
    (2) The purpose of the tithe (Acts 20:35)
    (3) The plea for the tithe (Mal. 3:10)

4. *The Cooperative Program and Your Stewardship*
    (1) Definition of the term
    (2) Description of the plan
    (3) Deepening appreciation (1 Cor. 1:10)

5. *Your Church and Your Stewardship*
    (1) A worthy budget for missions and local expenses (1 Cor. 14:40)
    (2) An enlistment program to reach each new member (Ex. 18:20)
    (3) Increase percentage of budget for Cooperative Program (2 Cor. 9:6)

Chapter 4 *Your Stewardship*

QUESTIONS FOR DISCUSSION

Chapter 4

1. Discuss God's ownership of you and your world.
2. Aside from money, what possessions of your life are you expected to yield to Him?
3. Tell what tithing is and in what spirit it is to be practiced.
4. What is the Cooperative Program?
5. What goes with the money you give through your church Sunday by Sunday? Name at least five causes supported by your gifts.

COMMITMENT

For the New Church Member

Believing that God owns the world in which I live, and knowing that He is the Lord and Master of my own life, I want my money as well as my life to honor Him. I will give gladly by God's plan that greater blessings from heaven may be mine.

(Signed) _____

Chapter 5

Your Life & Your Church

YOUR TESTIMONY

"Let the redeemed of the Lord say so" (Psalm 107:2). This verse expresses the urge of the Christian to tell others about his Lord. It tells of his obligation to share his own experience of conversion with others. Witnessing is as natural to the Christian as breathing. Conversion is such a glorious spiritual experience that one cannot remain quiet about it. It is so real that it must be revealed.

There is no such thing in the plan of God as secret discipleship. Jesus wants His disciples to be spokesmen of truth. He requires that they be heralds of glad tidings. One who knows the Christian message must tell it. One true to Christ must proclaim the glad tidings abroad.

There is no greater wisdom than that which is shown through proper Christian testimony. The Bible says very simply, "He that winneth souls is wise" (Prov. 11:30). One who deals with souls is handling eternal treasures. One soul won to God is more precious than all the material wealth of Wall Street.

As a Christian you have a story to tell. No one will tell the story just like you can. There is someone who will hear your testimony who will not listen to the preacher or anyone else. That fact makes your testimony imperative and effective. It gives you a unique place in the winning of the lost and in carrying out the plan of God.

1. The Message Is Glorious
The most glorious message the world can hear concerns human salvation. Because sin is terrible, salvation of the soul is glorious. It is a message so important that it must be shared. To hoard truth is selfishness and sin.

(1) What man is saved from.—The Bible deals frankly with the fact of sin from which the sinner is saved. It tells of sin's nature, its influence, and its tragic consequences. The emphasis of the Bible, however, is not on sin. The emphasis of the Bible is salvation. The Bible describes sin fully and tragically for the purpose of magnifying the miracle of salvation which saves man from sin which is so prevalent and tragic.

(2) What man is saved for.—Luke 15 is typical of the Bible passages which describe the awfulness of sin in order to magnify the purpose and the glory of redemption. In that chapter a sheep was lost. The lostness of the sheep was real and pathetic. Having no sense of direction the sheep could not find its own way. It was found by one who knew the way and cared for the lost. The same lesson is given as the story of the lost coin is told. It tells of the coin's sad state. It was lost to the purpose of which it was made. Coins were made for use. This one was buried under the floor. When found, its purpose was restored. So are sinners lost to the purposes of God. When they are saved, they are saved to serve.

(3) What man is saved to.—The message of salvation is glorious. The Bible deals with sin in order that it might magnify the greatness of the God who can save sinners so lost. Sinners are unworthy. God is forgiving. In true love God reaches down to rescue and lift men high, save them completely, and use them effectively in His service. The ultimate purpose of redemption is seen when the saved souls are lifted into heaven for eternal glory in God's presence. Man, therefore, is saved from hell, for service, and to glory.

2. The Plan Is Clear

(1) Every Christian a witness.—"Ye shall be witnesses unto me" (Acts 1:8). Many such passages of Scripture express in a clear way the specific command of God to bear testimony of His saving grace. His orders have been given clearly. In no sense do we have the right to disregard or disobey His specific orders. We are understanding orders to share the message of truth with others. It is our duty to tell of God's plan for human redemption. Each one who knows the way is to tell to others that they, too, can know the secret. Every Christian is a witness.

(2) The example of Jesus.—The life of Jesus is an example and a challenge for us to follow in evangelism. We must know what Jesus did. We are to do likewise. He touched all types of people and pointed them to the greatest truth of the ages—the truth of human salvation (Matt. 4:23; John 4:5-26). He considered salvation the most important message men can hear. He shared it in love and compassion. The Master's earthly life was spent in wooing and winning men to God. Salvation was His main mission and message.

(3) Witnessing by early disciples.—The early disciples took the Master seriously. They witnessed even at tremendous cost to themselves. So must we. When threatened with death for continuing to tell others of salvation, they merely replied, "We ought to obey God rather than men" (Acts 5:29). Christian testimony can be costly. It can cost us in ridicule, imprisonment, and in extreme instances death. Still the Commander is clear in His orders. We cannot afford to be silent concerning His purpose of coming, whatever the cost to us.

3. The Task Is Tremendous

(1) Geographical area to be covered.—"They ... went everywhere preaching the word" (Acts 8:4).

When a man builds a house, he can arrive at the place of driving his last nail and brushing his last bit of paint. He can then say, "It is a finished job." The Christian can never reach that place of completion in his Christian work. It is always an unfinished task. It is more like breathing or eating. Those things are in process but are never completely finished while life lasts.

Witnessing must be to all nations. God's saving grace is not limited to any particular color or nationality. Jesus witnessed to the woman of Samaria (John 4:7) and to the Syrophenician woman (Mark 7:26). They were both foreign to His own nation and people. He had to disregard the prejudices of His day in order to witness to them. Custom would have restrained Him. It is not always easy to witness to other peoples. Especially is this true when nations are on bad diplomatic relations. Peter had difficulty getting his own consent to witness to Cornelius (Acts 10:28). Paul was condemned for preaching to the Gentiles (Acts 15:1-2). As long as Christ's commission stands, however, we are to go to "all nations." Color lines and geographical boundaries must not limit the area for Christian testimony.

(2) Language barriers to be overcome.—Languages constitute a real difficulty in giving Christian testimony. It is not easy to preach to a man who does not understand your own tongue. Pentecost predicted triumph over this barrier when under the Holy Spirit's leadership people spoke in the languages of many nations of the wonderful works of God (Acts 2:11). The Bible has been translated into hundreds of languages for use today. The Bible speaks a common message to men's hearts everywhere regardless of the language used. God uses His Word in any and every language to reveal His will to the hearts of men. The Bible is a book that finds us wherever we are and speaks a personal message to us regardless of the language we speak.

(3) All types of people to be included.—The Bible portrays the necessity for witnessing to all types of people. Noble Nicodemus, the poor widow, the blind beggar, and the rich fool all heard Jesus' message. No person was too rich. None was too poor. Never was one too highly educated. Never was one too illiterate. No man was too moral to need Jesus. No person was too immoral for Jesus to cleanse. Jesus dealt with all people at all levels of earthly living. Spiritually they all stood alike before Him. He knew the universal needs of men. He knew that all men sinned regardless of economic or intellectual levels. He dealt with all age groups. He talked to those who were old. On his knees He held little children as He tried to influence their young hearts in love so that they would be willing to trust in Him when at a later time they would come to sense their inner spiritual needs.

All generations of men must be won. The task is endless. Were the whole earth reached in our generation, the task would not yet be completed. The whole world must be won all over again in every generation. Redeemed men pass from the scene. Others are born to live. They, too, must be saved. The task is as endless as the stream of human life itself. "The field is the world" (Matt. 13:38) and the continuous task of the Christian is "unto the end of the world" (Matt. 28:20) and to the end of time.

4. The Opportunities Are Challenging

With every Christian a witness, each day affords many opportunities to win souls to Christ. Even the most difficult circumstances can be overcome if hearts are sincere and Christian lives are dedicated.

(1) Among friends and acquaintances.—Every Christian has friends. Sometimes those friends are next of kin. That very kinship affords opportunity. Andrew won Peter his brother through direct testimony (John 1:40). Through that testimony he did more through one who was won than he could have accomplished through his own personal life in many years. Peter has become better known than Andrew, the man who won him to Jesus. But we could never say that Peter was greater than Andrew. They were great in different ways. Simple testimonies can be tremendously effective to close friends. For the Christian to say "I really do love Jesus" can work wonders under the guidance of the Holy Spirit when that testimony is given in sincerity to a close relative or friend. Testimony does not always have to be formal to be effective.

(2) In times of life's tragedies.—Grief affords an opportunity for meaningful Christian witnessing. Death strikes the home of a friend. Your help and kindness in that hour of sadness can speak volumes. Simple words, a helping hand, a tear of sympathy all declare a love and interest which God can use in leading people to accept your Christ. Since every man carries burdens too heavy to bear alone, there are limitless opportunities afforded Christians to witness in times of heartache. When tragedy comes your way, your own attitude in that time of grief can easily become the strongest Christian testimony your own life can give. Missionaries have learned that their courage and faith in times of grief on the mission field have done more to win heathens than many sermons. Paul's high conduct when he was imprisoned in Rome gave him a sympathetic audience who came to believe in the genuineness of his faith because of the way he faced his own life's trials.

Glorious spiritual experiences afford opportunities for evangelism. Peter at Pentecost (Acts 2:14) won many others to Christ by a simple gospel message. This testimony came just after he himself had experienced an unforgettable spiritual power which made him want to share his inner joy with others.

(3) Among chance acquaintances and passersby.—One of the important things to keep in mind is that opportunities pass hastily. The blind men by the wayside sensed their fleeting opportunity to be healed as Jesus passed by and they cried, "Thou Son of David, have mercy on us" (Matt. 9:27). Action is urgent when the door of opportunity is open. Those opportunities pass speedily. Today we may win a soul to Christ. Tomorrow that heart may be too hard. The last opportunity might be passed. Life itself might be ended. Action without delay is imperative.

5 The Methods Are Varied

(1) Formal and informal witnessing.—When we refer to witnessing, most people think of formal witnessing to others. By that we mean the making of a specific visit for the avowed purpose of talking with someone about his acceptance of Christ. That is a tremendously effective method of visitation. It must always be done after much prayer and under the leadership of the Holy Spirit. It must be carried on in sincerity and with the full use of God's Word. When such visitation is done systematically and in the spirit of Christ, the accomplishments are amazingly successful. Every church should continue a sustained program of witnessing for the sake of its own members as well as for the benefit of those who would be visited. Both the visitor and the visited are helped when Christians go out to witness.

Informal witnessing is also very effective. It is done more by the general spiritual tone of one's life in daily living. A passing remark or an unconscious influence as two people work side-by-side in the same factory or at the same desk may point another to Jesus. A wife may witness effectively to a hardhearted husband by the radiance of her own Christian life in times of hardship and heartache. A child can live in consecration before a hardhearted parent so that God can use that devotion to break the heart of a wayward father. Every deed of every Christian's life is a testimony. Such testimony should always remind others of Jesus. Some of the most effective witnessing is informally done as people live in the spirit of Christ and let their lives endlessly declare a faith in an allegiance to Christ. The world cannot escape or quickly forget such testimony.

(2) Special evangelistic meetings.—Testimony in times of special meetings should be done in a special way. When our church

schedules a revival meeting all other matters should be laid aside for an all-out endeavor in evangelism. If the churches of a city join in a special simultaneous soul-winning crusade, the Christians should clear their calendars of all competing events and activities. If church members go about their routine tasks during a revival meeting and do little about attendance on the evangelistic services or concern for the lost, the world gets the impression that those persons are insincere. This makes the testimony of those church members weaker if not ineffective.

A study will show that most Christians are won to Christ during revival meetings. That very fact proves the true worth of revivals. The simultaneous revival which unites many churches in evangelistic efforts in a whole city or county can give an impact upon that area which sinful hearts cannot ignore. Never is there a greater time of witnessing than during revival meetings and special evangelistic crusades.

(3) Perennial evangelism.—Regular Sunday-by-Sunday testimony by the pastor, Sunday School teachers, Discipleship Training leaders, and church officers helps build an endless program of evangelism which leads people to Christ and salvation the year around. Sinners are won around the clock and calendar because Christians are ever busy at the major task of ceaseless soul-winning. This method is called perennial evangelism. Truly it is a wonderful way to reach the lost. "And the Lord added to the church daily" (Acts 2:47) shows the constant achievements of Spirit-led evangelism.

Regular church services afford marvelous opportunity for evangelism. Evangelism should always be church centered. The church helps build the spirit, incentive, organization, and program of evangelism. It provides the list of prospects. Church-centered evangelism is New Testament evangelism at its best.

6. *The Rewards Are Many*

(1) A deeper faith.—Witnessing is telling what one knows to be true from his own personal experience. One cannot truthfully witness about hearsay things. When Jesus said, "Ye shall be witnesses unto me" (Acts 1:8), He was saying that He did not want Christians to maintain a selfish secrecy about the wondrous things Jesus has

done. He wants Christians to tell what they know by experience. It is to be told that lost people may come to know also. One of the rewards of the Christian is that he loves Christ more dearly when he shares his Christian experience with others. The more Christ is shared, the more real He is. The more a witness tells others of Jesus, the more of Jesus he possesses in his own heart. The more one proclaims the message of salvation, the more glorious that salvation experience becomes to him. It is another illustration of the principle that when one freely gives he freely receives.

(2) Happiness in the heart.—True Christian joy comes through seeing lives changed. There is tremendous delight in seeing the actual and immediate results of evangelism. When Jesus stopped to witness to the woman at the well of Sychar, He was physically tired (John 4:6). He was also very hungry. When He won the woman from her evil and sinful living, His own physical hunger was gone (John 4:32). He had a satisfaction in His own heart which could not be provided by food and water.

When the Christian wins another to faith in Christ and leads him to unite with the church for baptism and service, he feels the deepest spiritual joy imaginable. It is a happiness deep within the soul. A changed life is in itself a tremendous compensation for one's evangelistic efforts. It is wonderful for one to know that God has used him to witness to the heart and lives of others and to produce an eternal change in them for good. As you engage in evangelism you are participating in a partnership with God which is real and genuine.

(3) The praise of the Master.—The praise of Jesus will be reward enough for any Christian. When he comes to the end of the way and hears Jesus say "Well done" (Matt. 25:21) his heart receives all the reward one desires. Such a commendation from our Lord will compensate for all the criticisms and hardships that have come along that Christian's way. He will forget the rebuffs, persecutions, and cursings of men. He will be happily aware of the voice of praise from the great Master. That is all the reward that any Christian could really ask.

The task of witnessing must be done hastily. The urgency of the task of witnessing is shown in the words of Jesus, "Go out quickly . . .

and bring in hither the poor" (Luke 14:21). These words suggest the hurry which must be ours in the task of winning others. As food is needed for the body and medicine is demanded for the hospital, so Christ is urgently needed in human experience.

For one to succeed in evangelism costs much in effort and self-denial. Selfishness must be laid aside. Long hours must be spent in prayer. The Bible must be learned and loved. Attention must center on Christ and His eternal will. As the self is emptied of the things of the world, Christ fills us with the things of heaven in order that our testimonies might be effective. The testimony of the spiritual Christian becomes a mighty instrument in the hand of God for changing the world.

The art of soul-winning must be mastered by practice more than study. In one's first efforts to win the lost, mistakes will likely be made. The greatest mistake one can make is not to witness at all. Do not let the fear of making mistakes keep you from telling others of Jesus. Pray, witness with a compassionate heart, and trust everything else to Jesus. His Word will cut sinful hearts like a two-edged sword. Strong men will drop to their knees in repentance as God guides your words from dedicated lips to hungering hearts and listening ears. God will reward the simplest words and smallest deeds of the humblest Christian with mighty results. Eternal salvation will come to those who hear and heed as Christian truth is shared by those who know and love Christ.

SUMMARY OF CHAPTER 5
YOUR TESTIMONY

Introduction

1. *The Message Is Glorious*
    (1) What man is saved *from* (Matt. 1:21)
    (2) What man is saved *for* (1 Tim. 1:16-19)
    (3) What man is saved *to* (Rev. 21:1-3)

2. *The Plan Is Clear*
    (1) Every Christian a witness (Acts 1:8)
    (2) The example of Jesus (Matt. 4:23; John 4:5-26)
    (3) Witnessing by early disciples (Acts 5:29-32)

3. *The Task Is Tremendous*
    (1) Geographical area to be covered (Matt. 13:38)
    (2) Language barriers to be overcome (Acts 2:11)
    (3) All types of people to be included (John 3:1; Mark 10:46)

4. *The Opportunities Are Challenging*
    (1) Among friends and acquaintances (John 1:40)
    (2) In times of life's tragedies (Luke 7:12-15)
    (3) Among chance acquaintances and passersby (Matt. 9:27)

5. *The Methods Are Varied*
    (1) Formal and informal witnessing (Acts 4:8-13)
    (2) Special evangelistic meetings (2 Tim. 4:2)
    (3) Perennial evangelism (Acts 2:47)

6. *The Rewards Are Many*
    (1) A deeper faith (Acts 8:39)
    (2) Happiness in the heart (John 4:32)
    (3) The praise of the Master (Matt. 25:21)

Chapter 5 *Your Testimony*

QUESTIONS FOR DISCUSSION

CHAPTER 5

1. Why does Jesus save people?
2. Why do you think Jesus wants you to be a soul-winner?
3. What is a witness? How can you be one?
4. Discuss some of the difficulties in evangelism.
5. Tell the rewards awaiting you for faithfulness in soul-winning.

COMMITMENT

For the New Church Member

Knowing that Jesus is the only Saviour of the world, I dedicate myself now to the task of telling lost people about Him and His saving power. It is my prayer that God may use my lips and my life to direct wayward people to Him. It is my conviction that life can have no greater mission or purpose.

(Signed) _____

Chapter 6

Your Life & Your Church

YOUR HOME AND YOUR CHURCH

The home and the church are institutions of God, begun by His divine hands. They fulfill holy missions. Each plays an important role in your life, growth, and influence. Because God began both of these important institutions they are expected to serve Him as well as bless you. The home and the church are to work side-by-side in complete harmony of spirit and attitude. Each is to strengthen and encourage the other that the highest purposes of God might be served.

Already we have studied about the church. We have thought of its origin, beliefs, work, and importance. Now we center our attention on the home. This chapter is given with the prayer that the will of God shall be fully understood and completely done with regard to your home. You will find your deepest happiness as your home and your church work together to find and fulfill the purpose of the Creator and the mission of the Saviour.

1. Your Life and Your Home

Many times new Christians have transformed their own homes as their partnership with Christ became real. Having a deep desire to follow Him, they have influenced their entire families to be more Christlike. By suggestion and influence they have led parents and relatives to cooperate in making the home Christian in character and influence. Like leaven in a lump, the influence of these new Christian lives has mellowed the hearts of all other members of the family. They have changed the whole tone of the family's living by their own sweet Christian spirits. Marvelous is the influence of one consecrated Christian in any home. When all of the members of a family are Christian and Christlike, it is next to heaven.

Think of some of the things to be included in a successful family life:

(1) Private devotions.—Food for the body is necessary. Wholesome nourishment for the soul is just as essential. The quiet of the home is the best place for one's private devotions and silent moments with God. These experiences nurture and sustain the soul for life's deepest needs. Each member of the family must read God's Word privately. Through the Bible, as by the Spirit, God speaks to us. Family members need to pray individually. The reading of the Bible and the practice of daily prayers will strengthen each member of the family. It is wonderful when this is included as a regular part of the daily schedule of each member of the family. The new Christian should practice the quiet period of prayer and Bible study. He should invite the other members of the family to join him in that important practice. A Christian home is conducive to this spirit of private worship.

(2) Family worship.—Simple little things influence home life tremendously. The saying of thanks at meals is one of them. A husband or a wife can perhaps establish the practice of giving thanks before meals as a regular part of every day's schedule and practice. A child can always thank God quietly even though other members of the family may not be Christians. He can encourage other members of the family to join him in his daily expression of thanks before meals. Even though family members may not be Christians, it is possible that they can be influenced to cooperate in this desirable and worthwhile practice. If the family declines to join openly in the thanksgivings before meals, one can still do so privately. He can also make the resolution in his own heart that when his own home is established in later years he will make the prayers of thanksgiving a vital part of each day's practice. It is so much easier to establish the habit of praying in the home when that home is first begun.

Just before meals is a wonderful time to recall the blessings of God and thank Him for daily food. God is the giver "of every good and perfect gift" (James 1:17). Christians should acknowledge those blessings with daily thanksgiving. Human hearts become cold unless Christians recall the source of life's blessings and regularly thank the Giver of them. Few things are more tragic than for people to receive abundant favors from God and never feel or express thanks to Him for them. It is a glorious thing for families to join hearts and voices in acknowledging and thanking God for all of life's good things.

Chapter 6 *Your Home and Your Church*

One of the most beautiful acts of worship in the home is when members of the family join together in home worship with the father and mother leading and all members of the family sympathetically participating. These worship periods do not need to be long to be meaningful and effective. Family worship is at its best just before or just after one of the daily meals when the entire family is present in the home and can jointly participate. It would be at the same hour each day, if possible. With one member of the family reading the Scripture, another commenting on it, and still another leading the prayer, the entire family can actively participate in the significant family worship experiences. Members of the family can make informal comments or ask questions. They can sing together if they are musically inclined. These things invite group participation. They produce greater blessings and happiness. The old saying "The family that prays together stays together" is ever true.

Private devotions or family worship are not to serve as substitutes for worship in the church. Such acts only deepen the ability of the family to worship when Sunday does come. The home is not to compete with the church. Each is to supplement and strengthen the other. The two are not competitors. They are partners.

(3) *Wise guidance.*—Every home needs to provide helpful guidance to members of the family. Every day brings important decisions as the problems in human living are faced. The home can mean much by giving guidance as these important decisions are made by the family members. This guidance can be given in some measure by careful selection of good literature. Such literature can be purchased or selected from the church or community library. Since one becomes a part of what he reads, it is very necessary that the literature of the home be selected with great care. Books and magazines should be chosen with caution and wisdom since many of them can be detrimental to spiritual and emotional health. The alert parent tries to guide the child in the careful choice of reading matter. Good missionary and current magazines, the state Baptist paper, *HomeLife,* and other publications which contribute vitally to wholesome family living should be provided. Careful guidance should be given in the selection of radio and television programs. Even the recreational lives of the youngsters should have wise and sometimes firm guidance.

2. The Church Ministers to the Home

There is much the church can do as it fulfills its New Testament mission. It must seek to build stronger Christians through better Christian homes. Your church can be significant as it guides the home.

(1) In answering life's questions.—This is done through sermons, Sunday School lessons, discipleship studies, Woman's Missionary Union materials, Baptist Men on Mission discussions, and various other ministries and special instructions. The Bible is the true textbook of life, dealing with all areas of human living. The Bible tells how homes are to be established. It describes the family and home relationships that must exist. As the Bible is taught and heeded, the home is guided and strengthened.

One needs to know God's design for the home. He must understand how one is to prepare for Christian marriage. He must be aware of the necessity for clean moral living if the home is to be stable and secure. One needs to be warned of the dangers which the home must inevitably face as it competes with many evil forces in the modern workaday world. The lurking dangers which seek to destroy the spiritual lives of the members of the family must be kept ever before the members of the family that they may be prepared to face and withstand them. Recognizing the potential enemies of the home can help it gain many victories.

Through special study courses and conferences on Christian home life and through Christian Home Emphasis each year, many families can see their needs and opportunities in the building of better and stronger homes.

(2) When crises and victories come.—Human living inevitably brings joys and sorrows. It also brings defeats and victories. One cannot live long without being aware of both its hardships and delights. Life is that way. Christians are to live their lives beside other men in the same kind of world. They are to face the selfsame hardships.

When sickness comes or death is near, the church stands ready to comfort and help. Hardship provides the church a glorious opportunity for a special ministry in the home. Life's lessons through hardships may be hard, but they are lasting and meaningful. God has often taught us the meaning of Christian friendship and the value of Christian fellowship by bringing us face to face with some hard experiences of life. It is then that we can appreciate the church fully and realize what it has to afford us in hours of greatest need. A church must never miss that opportunity of helping others in time of distress or disaster.

The church guides younger members of the home in their choice of vocations. God has a special place of service for every life. There is some one place where each person can serve Him best. Rare temperaments and abilities were given each individual by God for a special purpose. The wide-awake church helps its young people find those places of greatest service. It is only when this discovery has been made that they can find happiness through real achievement. Vocational guidance is a significant church opportunity that will pay huge dividends in human happiness and usefulness.

When a family moves from one city to another or even from community to community, the home experiences a tremendous shock. It is impossible to move a family geographically without causing difficult readjustment. Friends of long standing are left behind. Patterns of life are suddenly and drastically altered. Adjustments must be made to new schools, new friends, and new jobs. At a time of readjustment like that the church can be of special assistance to the family and the home. The best way for a family to adjust in the new community is under the guidance and with the help of the Baptist church where the family has just moved. A group of special friends awaits each member of the family within that church. The family can soon adjust to its new situation with the sympathetic encouragement of newfound church friends. The helpful guidance of a sincere and wide-awake church means much. This fact makes it urgent that the members of a family move their church letters immediately upon moving to a new community. They should seek the church. They should not wait for the church to seek them. The ideal is when the seeking Christian and the seeking church meet halfway.

The church will be near in time of rejoicing as well as in the hour of sorrow or perplexity. When a member of the family marries or graduates, the church is near to share in the rejoicing. When there is a conversion in the family or a special honor to come to some member of the family, the church finds itself exceedingly happy over that victory or achievement. When a new baby is born, the church looks upon its birth as a special occasion in the life of that family and lays appropriate plans to help. The church provides immediately for more facilities and leadership that the child might be wisely nurtured and spiritually guided from its earliest days.

While infants are too young to be converted, they are never too young to be influenced and impressed in spirit and attitude. They can be made to feel that they are welcome and wanted from earliest days. The wide-awake church seeks to give careful instruction and guidance to the little child from its youngest years. In that way conversion will come easier when the age of accountability is reached. When a child is properly cared for in the church, his two parents are more closely linked to the church. Few things will enlist parents quicker in church life than adequate provision for wise religious training of their child.

(3) Through constant guidance and inspiration.—It is wonderful to see families sitting together during church worship services. During Sunday School they have met by age groups. During church services it is well for them to sit in family groups, if possible. It makes a tremendous impact on the entire family when all the members sit together during the church services. They are helped greatly when they sing, pray, and worship side-by-side. It is also a silent testimony to others that the home is dedicated to the glorious spiritual purposes of God.

The church in planning its program provides for each member of the family regardless of age or circumstances. Family participation is provided by the church in Sunday School, Discipleship Training, and Music Ministry. It is easier to keep the standards of speech high and the morality of the family acceptable to God and the community when that family is regular in church worship.

3. The Home Cooperates with the Church

Just as the church has a ministry to the home, so the home has an obligation to the church. It receives blessings from the church. In turn it must fulfill certain duties to the church.

(1) By important religious instruction.—The setting aside of sufficient time for church services and worship is a duty of the home.

Immature children cannot wisely schedule their hours and days without cautious parental guidance. In the crowded schedules of modern-day living, community pressures are so great that the youngsters can easily but unconsciously crowd Christian training out of their lives if the parents carelessly allow it. It is easy to let the good become an enemy of the best. Even worthwhile things should never crowd out the best things. It is the duty of the home to schedule activities for all members of the family so as to guarantee proper spiritual guidance for each family member until maturity.

(2) Through the practice of stewardship.—Training in giving is a home duty. All Christians should recognize the necessity for regular giving to the kingdom enterprises. Christ expects it. God provided a plan of stewardship. In chapter 4 we studied that Christian principle. Christians recognize and practice God's plan of regular proportionate and joyful giving. The emphasis here is to stress the necessity for participation by each member of the family in the plan of church giving. The giving should not be done by father and mother alone. Family giving should be engaged in regularly by each member of the family. It is a matter of necessary training. Training in giving is a home responsibility which must not be neglected. Giving is an act of worship. It expresses gratitude to God. It helps the growing Christian to properly evaluate the church. If more money goes to the theatre from the child than goes to the church, that child is likely to think that a theatre is more important than the church. Giving declares that the church is important and worthy of one's best. Regular giving helps members of the family make week-by-week investments in the finer things of life through the church. It helps them experience the thrill of participation in a worldwide program of missions and benevolence. Because of the joys that come through giving, the father and mother should provide ways and means by which each child can give each Sunday through the church. In this way the child gives to all the causes of the kingdom of God.

(3) In the development of talents for special services.—The dedication of talents should also be under family guidance. If one member of the family can sing well, it is the duty of the home to guide that child in full participation and training in religious music. The home should see to it that every opportunity is afforded that child through the church's age-group choir. Some member of each family has outstanding potentialities for teaching, organizing, visitation, ministry

to the needy, or some other special service to the community. Here is an area in which the home can give helpful assistance as it guides the family members in training for places of highest service in the life of the church.

The home of the Christian can also be used for special meetings by the church and church groups. Prayer services, recreational gatherings, and fellowship meetings must be held in homes which are usable for good Christian purposes. It is a tragedy when parents consider a home so expensively furnished that it cannot be used as an instrument of God for special guidance in the spiritual growth of the members of the family. Blessed is that home whose doors are always open for use in meeting the needs of the church upon the request of the pastor or church organizations.

4. Building Christian Homes for Today

Today's homes need to be stronger than ever. Never have the enemies of the home been stronger. Forces of evil in these times are so tremendous that home life in America cannot possibly survive unless it is undergirded by strong Christian forces and influence.

(1) Essential to world evangelization.—The winning of a child to Christ from a Christian home is much easier than the winning of one who has lived in a non-Christian environment. This is an established fact. It has been the experience of every soul-winner. A child who is familiar with Bible teaching from earliest years catches a spirit and knows certain truths which are conducive to a deep soul experience. Certain fundamental knowledge is necessary to the Christian experience of conversion (Rom. 10:14). That knowledge can be received through the testimony of godly parents as well as Christian ministers and witnesses. When one is reared in an environment of love and is taught the Bible from earliest years, he has a receptive attitude which lends itself to an earlier and easier conversion experience when the age of accountability arrives. The home plays a tremendous part in instructing the child aright. Thousands of Christian homes so dedicated can make an impact upon the spiritual life of the whole earth in our time.

(2) Necessary to national security.—In our effort to build a greater national stability, we must not overlook the special contributions

made by the Christian home. It is a very important and necessary unit in the security and survival of our nation. The Christian home also adds much to the prosperity of our whole national life. As the home goes, so goes the nation. The very worst potential enemy of the nation is not from without. It is from within. Quickest defeat can come from disintegration and neglect of American homes. The subtlety of such an attack makes the present condition serious indeed. Christian forces must awaken to arise and build strong Christian homes today. In doing so they will make a contribution to the moral tone of the age. At the same time they are rendering a tremendous service in making the nation stable and strong. Homes can become better as Christians give themselves in conscientious devotion to the fine art of Christian home building. A nation is no stronger than its homes. Homes are just as stable as the people who make up the family.

(3) In it all Christ is honored.— We are trying to serve Christ in the building of homes which are shaped by heaven's design. Parents are to sense their Christian duty. They are to give correct example, instruction, and inspiration. Children are to accept their own part of the responsibility by following parental guidance, and honoring their fathers and mothers in every way possible.

What is more beautiful than a home completely dedicated to the service of God through the church? It is one of earth's most significant scenes. It is one of heaven's greatest gifts. All of us must recognize the definite need for immediate attention to this most pressing problem. Christ will bless our efforts as we try to honor Him by guiding homes according to the plan of God. As Christian homes are built, Christ will get the glory.

The world stands in need of men today like Joshua of old, who said in fervent devotion, "As for me and my house, we will serve the Lord" (Josh. 24:15). Such fathers with similar dedication and purpose can change the world. First, there must be a solid resolution that God's will shall be fully done in the lives of parents. The homes must be dedicated. The children must be wisely guided and cautiously instructed. Prayer and Bible reading must make regular contributions. Success comes as homes match the noble opportunity of the present hour with dedicated Christian living on the part of every member of every family.

SUMMARY OF CHAPTER 6
Your Home and Your Church

Introduction

1. *Your Life and Your Home*
   (1) Private devotions (Matt. 6:6)
   (2) Family worship (Deut. 6:6-9; Eph. 5:20)
   (3) Wise guidance (Prov. 22:6)

2. *The Church Ministers to the Home*
   (1) In answering life's questions (Prov. 23:22-26)
   (2) When crises and victories come (John 11:14, 25-26)
   (3) Through constant guidance and inspiration (2 Tim. 1:5)

3. *The Home Cooperates with the Church*
   (1) By important religious instruction (1 Tim. 6:1-2)
   (2) Through the practice of stewardship (2 Tim. 2:15)
   (3) In the development of talents for special services (2 Tim. 2:2)

4. *Building Christian Homes for Today*
   (1) Essential to world evangelization (2 Tim. 1:5)
   (2) Necessary to national security (Psalm 33:12)
   (3) In it all Christ is honored (1 Cor. 10:31)

QUESTIONS FOR DISCUSSION

Chapter 6

1. Discuss the origin and influence of the home.
2. Tell the relation between the home and the church.
3. How can a new Christian influence his home for Christ?
4. What is a family altar?
5. How can your church minister to your home?

COMMITMENT

For the New Church Member

Feeling that I can honor Christ through Christian living in my home, I will do my best to make my home Christian. Through faith and right living I will try to influence my home so that it will always radiate the spirit and message of Jesus. I will seek to lead my family to join me in private devotions and a family altar so that Christ may ever be the honored guest in our home.

(Signed) _____

Chapter 7

Your Life & Your Church

YOUR ALL FOR CHRIST

From Christ you have received full forgiveness. In return you are asked to follow Him devotedly and serve Him faithfully. The manner in which you can please Him most is by dedicated faithfulness through the church.

Careless discipleship is not enough for Jesus. To be sure He came into the world to be your Saviour and Redeemer. He wants also to be Lord and Master (Acts 2:36) as well. Jesus is not unfair, therefore, in asking you to give your all for Him and His service. He first gave His all for you. He has a perfect right to ask in return that all of your life be given in consecrated service for His glory.

This chapter proposes to set forth the need for full dedication. It appeals for complete discipleship. It also tells the means by which you can render your most acceptable service to Him. It is a challenge that you as a Christian hold back nothing from Christ which He needs and can use. Only the fullest measure of your devotion will be pleasing to Him. Anything else is too small.

1. Christ's Example

(1) In righteous living.—No life has ever been as complete as the life of Jesus. He possessed everything. To observe Him is to look at perfect human living. Jesus came not only to reveal God to us, He came also to show us how we should live for Him. His life was without flaw. He "was in all points tempted like as we are, yet without sin" (Heb. 4:15). He was able to withstand every enticing appeal of the devil and remain pure in body and soul. He never stooped to do a little or questionable thing. He never sinned in His

entire lifetime. Jesus shut everything out of His life which would have been evil or even questionable. He possessed all that was good. He committed no sin of commission. He did not commit sins of omission. He refused to do that which was wrong. He did fully that which was right. His was a truly righteous life without flaw.

(2) In heartfelt compassion.—Perhaps the most outstanding characteristic of Jesus was love. Love explains every great deed in His noble life. Without love He could not have been the Saviour. He would never have consented to come to earth on His redeeming mission had He not first loved us. He had a deep love for mankind. To Him love was very real. It found the way for Him to help and rescue man.

Love brought Jesus to earth. It led Him to die for the world which His love had embraced. His love was not racial. It was not geographical. Nor was it limited to any one generation or civilization. His love led Him to understand the rich and sympathize with the poor. It led Him to provide a way of escape for the wise and the unwise. So deep was His affection that He suffered when humanity suffered. He put Himself literally in the place of an unfortunate humanity. He was well aware of every heart hunger and heartache. His own heart pained when humanity was in distress. The ability of Jesus to feel deep needs of humanity is called compassion. Jesus possessed that sympathetic feeling in its highest expression.

(3) In consecrated service.—Jesus' earthly ministry was demonstration of Christian service at its best. The people who were neglected most were also the ones whom Jesus most readily helped. Beggars by the wayside, lepers who were outcasts, foreigners who were despised—these were the ones Jesus stooped tenderly to help and heal. He came "not to be ministered unto, but to minister" (Matt. 20:28). In fulfillment of this high and holy purpose He demonstrated life's real mission and spirit.

(4) In voluntary sacrifice.—Christ's sacrifices were fully and freely made. Jesus experienced many of them even before He came to die on the cross. Leaving heaven was sacrifice within itself. He left behind Him the ivory palaces of heaven to dwell in a world of sin. What a downward step! That sacrifice was gladly endured that men

might be uplifted from the fallen world to join Jesus in heaven's eternal glories. His earthly poverty was also a sacrifice. What a contrast to heaven in riches and glories previously known. He was born in a stable, placed in a manger, wrapped in swaddling clothes, and carried as a babe into foreign exile. He knew hardship. He worked in a carpenter shop and died penniless. All of these handicaps indicated the depth and the sincerity of His compassion for mankind. Gethsemane, also, was a sacrifice. In that garden of prayer the full load of human sin was laid on the soul of Jesus. No wonder the anguish of the burden produced sweatdrops like unto blood (Luke 22:44). In some ways that anguish of Gethsemane was more intense than the sufferings of His death on Calvary. The sacrifice Jesus made which meant most to us was His death on the cross of Calvary. It was there that He showed the full measure of His deep devotion for mankind. The anguish and the shame of the cross were willingly endured that freedom and redemption might be purchased for our souls. We cannot think of love so deep without resolving to give utmost devotion to Him in return.

(5) In resurrected glory.—The enemies of Christ were determined to destroy Jesus. After slaying Him brutally and unjustly they were determined to make the burial of His body the end of His earthly life and influence. They laid the body of our Lord in a grave. They sealed it with a Roman seal. Desperately they were trying to make sure there would be no resurrection (Matt. 27:64). Every earthly force available to His enemies was dedicated to the effort of keeping Jesus in the grave. These obstacles only made the resurrection more real and glorious. Even the mighty force of a Roman army could not keep our Lord in a sealed tomb. Jesus came forth alive. He appeared to men. He encouraged His disciples. He baffled His enemies. The evidences of His resurrection are as numerous as the proofs of His death. He lives! He lives today. Living, the Master has promised to make His followers "more than conquerors" (Rom. 8:37). We are not laboring, therefore, in a defeated cause. We are participants in the one movement of earth which is destined to succeed. In the course of the years the church may know many difficulties and trials. In the end it will also know complete victory.

2. The World's Need

(1) Confusion and uncertainty.—Even the world's leaders today are baffled as they face the present clash of ideologies and systems of government. Newspaper headlines are bold and contradictory in their interpretations of world affairs. The wisest of men admit that no answer to the problem is found in education, better housing, or more rigid laws. Such efforts are noble but insufficient to change the basic problem of human sin. Without the Christian message such human efforts would only intensify our problems. It is well for us to remember that an educated criminal can be more subtle and elusive than one who is unschooled. Amid all the baffling confusions of the present hour, there is a heart yearning for something secure and firm. Our age wants a rock to which it can anchor in the present-day storm. It also wants an anchor which will hold.

(2) Hatred and strife.—The tensions of the world are at a white-hot heat. Nations are at each others' throats. Races despise other races. Professions are clashing and competing. Civilizations clash headlong in their struggle for power and mastery. It is a grapple unto death. Conflict characterizes our time. It is truly an era of crisis. That very fact makes the call for consecrated Christians more urgent. It makes your witness more needed and effective in this hour of urgent opportunity.

(3) Hunger and heartache.—The Bible describes the yearnings of the human soul with the words "hunger" and "thirst." Men's souls yearn and burn for God. The spirit of restlessness which is prevalent is evidence of unsatisfied desires. The human heart will hunger until it feeds on the bread of heaven. It will thirst until it drinks of the water of life. God uses these deep driving human desires to woo us into His presence and keep us near to Him. A relationship like that of the sheep to the shepherd is made necessary by the very circumstances of life.

(4) Lost and doomed.—The world is in its grief because it is a world of sin. Our world is experiencing turmoil and strife because Christ has been shut out. Men and nations have been willing to experiment with every imaginable human remedy. Superficial suggestions and synthetic remedies have been proposed. No human help has been found. Governments have taxed to the limit as they have tried

to secure money which might possibly supply the needs of a restless age. It has become obvious that the greatest needs are not material. It is impossible, therefore, for the desires of the human heart to be satisfied with material possessions. All men are aware of need. The problem is to get men to accept the remedy which God has provided. No man or agency of men can satisfy the longings of an anxious heart without God's help.

3. The Christian's Opportunity

(1) Christians have the answer.—We have found the source of supply for all human needs in Christ. He has saved our souls, anchored our lives, and given us the "peace that passeth understanding." Knowing the secret, it would be almost criminal for us to refuse to share it with others who need it desperately. What would the world's attitude toward Pasteur be when he made his marvelous scientific discoveries, which have saved thousands of lives, had he locked those secrets in a private vault? His discovery made it obligatory that he share the glad news with others. Christians are under even greater obligation to share the truths of God with sinful men. That sense of duty to a lost world was expressed by Paul's striking words, "I am debtor" (Rom. 1:14). He was duty bound to others because he himself had experienced salvation from God. A knowledge of truth made it necessary for him to share that truth with others who needed to know it. God ordered it. The entire life of the Christian must be given in partial payment of the soul's debt to God. You have been saved that others might know the Christ through you.

(2) The world admits its need.—This is the first step toward victory. Only the sick willingly accept the remedy of the physician. Sinners must be aware of sin before they are in a spirit to humble themselves and ask for God's mercy. That very fact is one of the brightest lights on today's horizon. The world is becoming aware of the shocking fact that something is basically wrong with human living. Knowledge of need is the first indication of the desire to receive. Many editorials, magazine articles, and platform addresses are admitting that the soul needs of humanity are staggeringly great. Even governmental leaders and international statesmen confess that God alone holds the key to our way of escape from our dilemma. That admission of need becomes our first expression of hope.

(3) Today is the day.—The world's sense of need is the signal which should trigger our all-out effort to win the world to Christ. The world's admission of need is our invitation to act now. All-out Christian discipleship on the part of Christians can mean as much now as at any time in the world's entire history. Tragic would it be for Christians to withhold testimony now awaiting a better day or a more strategic hour. Today is the day. This is the time (2 Cor. 6:2). To fail now is to fail utterly. It is to fail in our hour of greatest opportunity. Hesitation now would make our failure all the more shameful.

The devil seeks to produce indifference. He would try to take away our heart burdens for the lost. He attempts to make us complacent and self-satisfied. He would deafen our ears to humanity's cries. He would shut our eyes to their distress. The devil is always anxious to chill our spirits, cool our ardor, and paralyze our influence. In contrast, Christ's plan calls for immediate action. There is no place in His plan for hesitation or delay.

People without Christ are lost. They are tragically and pathetically lost. They are not irreparably lost if we as Christian people, moved by the Spirit of Christ, will labor diligently for their rescue and salvation.

4. The Immediate Urgency

(1) The forces of evil.—Mighty are the forces of evil which seek to stampede the world into idolatry and heathenism. On the surface, communism appears to be in the saddle riding triumphantly forward. Emphasizing its godless philosophy, it is trying to trample underfoot everything that is Christian and right. Its apparent progress in the last few years has been amazing and shocking. Its dark shadows seem to hover over many nations in this alarming hour. How are we to halt the parade of communism? Records of delinquency and crime also blacken the headlines of every day's newspaper. How are we to counteract the combined evil forces in the world of our day? The urgency of this problem is staggering. God help us to awaken now! We should awaken with determination and a prayer. Further delay will leave the door wide open for the world's evil forces to lash out fury and tragedy. Delay is detrimental and deadly.

(2) The enslavement of evil habits.—The longer we wait, the more serious is the problem of reaching people. Sins are enslaving. Little questionable habits which are cobwebs today can easily become cables tomorrow. Sinners become more firmly chained in the ways of the world. Delays in deliverance make rescue more difficult. Hesitation will lead us to encounter additional obstacles. The longer a sinner continues in his sin, the more seared his soul becomes. Years of dissipation and immorality make it more difficult for one to feel deep soul convictions which are necessary to salvation.

(3) The command of Christ.—Jesus had a right to demand our Christian best in devoted discipleship. His high expectations are expressed in the noble words, "He that taketh not his cross, and followeth after me, is not worthy of me" (Matt. 10:38). Christ had His cross. We also have ours. The command is clear. The expectations are high. We understand in our minds what He wants. It is a mere matter of our willingness to do that which we know in our souls to be His wise will.

(4) The brevity of life.—"The night cometh, when no man can work" (John 9:4). This is a wise warning. The sun shines today. In a few hours darkness falls. Our one and only chance of serving Him is when we are on the stage of earthly living. Then comes death and removes our opportunity forever. If we do not serve Christ during our earthly lives, our one chance to serve Him is past without recall. The Bible says, "David . . . served his own generation by the will of God, and fell on sleep" (Acts 13:36). Had David not served God in his own generation he would not have served him in any generation. Man's earthly life is his only opportunity. Earthly life is at best very short. This fact demands haste in the giving of full and complete discipleship.

A fireman cannot idle along when the city is burning. A conscientious doctor will not relax while a scourge is sweeping the city. So is the Christian's message urgent in our time.

5. Your All Through His Church

(1) Through ceaseless prayers.—Prayer is the means by which Christians receive God's help to live victoriously. It is the source of wisdom by which you can come to know God's will for your life. It

helps you meet the issues of life with victory. It keeps you on good terms of fellowship with God. It is through prayer that God's will becomes fully revealed to you. The secret of God's power is discovered by prayer. You are never higher than when you drop to your knees in prayer to God. Perhaps one of your greatest contributions is to pray for the pastor and all of the church activities and services. Samuel said after many years of governmental leadership, "God forbid that I should sin against the Lord in ceasing to pray for you" (1 Sam. 12:23). The prayers of the Bible are significant and varied. People prayed in every conceivable posture and under many different circumstances. Where they prayed aright, God was ready to listen. God gave the victory. The admonition of Paul, "Pray without ceasing" (1 Thess. 5:17), calls us to live in the eternal spirit of prayer.

(2) Through regular church worship.—Church attendance is a powerful Christian testimony. The world identifies you with the organizations of which you are a part. To be a part of the church is to be identified with earth's greatest institution. Your worship in the church should be regular and real. The soul needs constant nourishment, fellowship, strength, comfort, and opportunities of service. These are all afforded through your church as God's spirit leads. Much happiness becomes yours when you make your life an integral part of a New Testament church and its work.

(3) Through systematic teaching and training.—You should never miss Sunday School unless it is for some providential reason beyond your own control. The Sunday School is the church fulfilling its teaching obligation to your life. You should take full advantage of its instruction. As you become more familiar with the Bible and its full teachings, the church may want you to serve in some place of leadership. You may be needed as a teacher or an officer. Be resolved to be ready! Don't miss a single opportunity to train adequately for future leadership. The church doubtless needs you and your services.

The study of this book may be under the guidance of Discipleship Training. Already you should have enrolled in a group as you began the study of these significant chapters. Upon completion of this special study you should begin another discipleship study in a group at church. There you will be given the best guidance possible as you grow in grace and in the knowledge of the Lord and Saviour.

(4) Through cooperative endeavors.—You must learn to work and serve with others. While there is a definite place for private service to God, there is also the need for cooperative effort. The very existence of the church indicates that God wanted us to work and worship with others. Jesus began the church because there are things which can be accomplished by group action which could never be attained by individual effort. The church and its organizations help you as you work diligently by the side of others for the glory of the Master.

(5) Through faithful giving.—Giving provides some great thrills to the Christian. Already you should be putting your tithes into the church weekly. The giving of one tenth of your income will make you a very real part of the missionary program of your church. You will be delighted to know that you are participating in the many causes and programs for which you are responsible as a Christian. It will channel your contributions through your church and help humanity in all of its various needs. Let your giving be regular and through the church. Let those gifts be made in gladness.

(6) Through missionary service.—The Bible is filled with verses which reveal the extent of Christ's interest in the entire world and the Christian's responsibility. Jesus' love circles the globe. Words like "all men," "everywhere," "uttermost," "whosoever," show the compassion Christ had for all mankind. They indicate His interest in the entire world. As a follower of Jesus you too must love the world. You must keep informed about the progress of the great missionary enterprise of Baptists.

The International Mission Board of the Southern Baptist Convention, the North American Mission Board of the Southern Baptist Convention, and your own state mission board receive constant support through the Cooperative Program through which your gifts to your church are channeled week by week. This means that you are an active participant in worldwide missionary enterprise when you give through the Cooperative Program. It means that you are helping to care for orphans. You are ministering to the sick in the hospitals, caring for aged ministers, helping teach and train preachers and missionaries that they might render a better service. You are supporting outstanding missionary work upon which the sun never sets.

To be a Baptist is to be a missionary. The title "missionary Baptist" should be unnecessary. It is a superfluous term like "tooth dentist." If one is Baptist, he is missionary. No adjective or descriptive term is necessary. The Bible is a missionary book. As the Bible is taught and followed, missions must be believed and practiced. Baptists are missionary or they are not true Baptists.

Good works play a vital part in human happiness. By those works our rewards will be measured. How wonderful it is to be invited into endless partnership with Jesus and find our own lives enlarged by that fellowship in missionary endeavors.

The crowning climax of it all will come on the glorious day of Jesus' return to earth. When He calls the faithful ones to Himself, evaluates our good works, and sees our faithfulness, He will say, "Come unto me." His eternal presence will be our crowning reward for Christian faith and service.

SUMMARY OF CHAPTER 7

Your All for Christ

Introduction

1. *Christ's Example*
    (1) In righteous living (Heb. 4:15)
    (2) In heartfelt compassion (Matt. 9:36)
    (3) In consecrated service (Matt. 20:28)
    (4) In voluntary sacrifice (Isa. 53:7)
    (5) In resurrected glory (Matt. 28:6)

2. *The World's Need*
    (1) Confusion and uncertainty (John 14:5)
    (2) Hatred and strife (Matt. 24:6)
    (3) Hunger and heartache (1 Cor. 4:11)
    (4) Lost and doomed (Luke 19:10)

3. *The Christian's Opportunity*
    (1) Christians have the answer (Rom. 1:11)
    (2) The world admits its need (John 14:8)
    (3) Today is the day (2 Cor. 6:2)

4. *The Immediate Urgency*
    (1) The forces of evil (1 Peter 5:8)
    (2) The enslavement of evil habits (Eph. 6:12)
    (3) The command of Christ (Matt. 10:38)
    (4) The brevity of life (John 9:4; Heb. 9:27)

5. *Your All Through His Church*
    (1) Through ceaseless prayers (1 Thess. 5:17)
    (2) Through regular church worship (Heb. 10:25)
    (3) Through systematic teaching and training (2 Tim. 2:15)
    (4) Through cooperative endeavors (Eph. 2:19-22)
    (5) Through faithful giving (1 Tim. 6:17-19)
    (6) Through missionary service (1 Tim. 2:1-4)

QUESTIONS FOR DISCUSSION

Chapter 7

1. Show how Christ's example should inspire us in service to needy humanity.
2. Discuss the dire spiritual needs of the world today.
3. Describe the urgency of sharing the Christian message now.
4. Tell how the church can help you in your service to Christ.
5. Discuss any special benefits you have received from this study.

Chapter 7 *Your All for Christ*

MY COMMITMENT: MY ALL FOR CHRIST

I made a public profession of faith in Jesus Christ as my personal Saviour on _____. I was baptized by _____ on _____ and was received into the full fellowship of the _____ Baptist Church, located at _____. I am now a member of the _____ Baptist Church at _____, and my pastor is _____.

I have finished the study of this book, and have signed the personal commitments of dedication at the close of the chapters. I come now to make a glad commitment of my all for Christ.

Because my Lord has done so much for me, it is my purpose of heart to come into His presence daily in prayer and Bible study. I will follow Him to the utmost in home life, church life, and everyday Christian witnessing.

I gladly pledge at least one tenth of my income for His work.

It is my purpose, with God's help, to be faithful in attendance upon the worship and prayer services of my church, to be a faithful member of Sunday School, of Discipleship Training, and of any other organizations of my church for which I am eligible.

"I press toward the mark for the prize of the high calling of God in Christ Jesus" (Phil 3:14).

(Signed) _____

Teaching Helps

GENERAL SUGGESTIONS

1. Enroll all new church members in New Member Training. Give to each one a copy of this book, Sunday School and Discipleship Training literature appropriate for his age group, and *HomeLife*. When orientation is done in a group, record and report attendance only.

2. New Member Training should continue as a group or a personal conference without a break as long as one new member has not completed it. Furthermore, it should begin for each member immediately after he joins the church. If necessary, seek through personal conferences to assure him and the church of his conversion and commitment. Then let him enter New Member Training at the session the group is studying at the time. Upon completing the last session, he can then continue with the leader until he has had the sessions he missed at the beginning of the course.

3. The purpose of this book can best be accomplished when the pastor is the leader. In some cases it will be found desirable to have several groups, graded by departments and meeting simultaneously.

4. Let the study be more of a discussion than a lecture.

5. Use chalkboard, charts, and pictures freely.

Teaching Helps

CHAPTER 1

1. Have each member relate his experience of conversion simply. He needs to be trained in the art of testimony and witnessing.

2. Distribute tracts on soul-winning (available at your state convention office) with the insistence that each new church member seek to lead someone to Christ.

3. Make the study simple enough that the youngest member will understand and be helped by the contents of this book.

4. Have members memorize Scripture verses which tell the duration of salvation. The new convert needs assurance. The Bible can help tremendously at that point.

CHAPTER 2

1. Impress upon the members that the church is made up of the people. It is not the building in which the people meet.

2. Discuss the government's scorn of soldiers who go AWOL (absent without leave). Discuss God's concern when Christian seek to get forgiveness but do not desire to give discipleship.

3. Suggest tangible ways in which the members may prove their love and loyalty to the church.

4. Request the members to list some definite objectives for the church in evangelism, stewardship, or missions.

Teaching Helps

CHAPTER 3

1. Ask the Sunday School director, Discipleship Training director, Woman's Missionary Union director, Women's Ministry director, Men's Ministry director and Baptist Men on Mission director to be present. Introduce them personally to the new church members.

2. Check names of all new church members against the organization rolls to see if they have been enlisted in the organizations for which they are eligible.

3. See if the church will agree to present Bibles that are in good condition or Testaments for free distribution to new members who do not have Bibles. A personal word from the pastor may be profitably inserted on the flyleaf.

4. Take new members on a tour of the church property, explaining the purpose and function of each area of the building.

5. Have maps of the association, state convention, Southern Baptist Convention and world to show the denominational relationship of your church to all Baptist life in the world.

CHAPTER 4

1. Display and analyze the budget of your own church.

2. Study the budgets for your state Baptist convention and the Southern Baptist Convention.

3. Choose, evaluate, discuss, and distribute appropriate stewardship tracts.

4. Have a world map, pinpointing the areas of work of the North American and International Mission boards.

5. Have pictures of all Baptist schools and orphanages in your state to display. Discuss in the group the work of Christian education.

CHAPTER 5

1. Organize visitation teams so that young Christians can learn to witness with the assistance of more experienced church leaders.

2. Select some good Bible verses to be used by young Christians in witnessing. Discuss these verses fully during group time.

3. Show some of the necessary steps in soul-winning. Warn against the things that are to be avoided in evangelism, such as argument.

4. Provide evangelistic tracts for distribution. Tell how wisest use of tracts can be made.

CHAPTER 6

1. Have some copies of *HomeLife* for free distribution to all members.

2. Give a demonstration of a properly conducted family devotional.

3. Select Scripture references showing Christ's interest in the home and His contributions to it.

4. Seek to determine the number of group members who are reading the Bible daily in private devotion in the home.

5. Introduce one of the outstanding Christian families of the church to your group. Let the members of that family take a couple of minutes to tell what the church means to their home.

Teaching Helps

CHAPTER 7

1. Have a member clip newspaper and magazine articles of the previous week which indicate the deep spiritual needs of the world.

2. Use the Bible to show that Christ has the answer to each of the aforementioned personal, social, or political problems.

3. Find references in the Bible showing the many times Jesus was willing to give His time in service to meet the spiritual needs of His day.

4. List specific examples of Christian service which can be done today by each member of the group.

5. Assign each new member to an appropriate Sunday School class and Discipleship Training group.

CHRISTIAN GROWTH STUDY PLAN

Preparing Christians to Serve

In the **Christian Growth Study Plan (formerly Church Study Course)**, this book *Your Life and Your Church* is a resource for course credit in the subject area Church of the Christian Growth category of diploma plans. To receive credit, read the book, complete the learning activities, show your work to your pastor, a staff member or church leader, then complete the following information. This page may be duplicated. Send the completed page to:

Christian Growth Study Plan
One LifeWay Plaza
Nashville, TN 37234-0117
FAX: (615)251-5067
Email: *cgspnet@lifeway.com*
For information about the Christian Growth Study Plan, refer to the Christian Growth Study Plan Catalog. It is located online at *www.lifeway.com/cgsp*. If you do not have access to the Internet, contact the Christian Growth Study Plan office (1.800.968.5519) for the specific plan you need for your ministry.

Your Life and Your Church
COURSE NUMBER: CG-0423

PARTICIPANT INFORMATION

Social Security Number (USA ONLY)	Personal CGSP Number*	Date of Birth (MONTH, DAY, YEAR)
- -	-	- -

Name (First, Middle, Last)	Home Phone
	-

Address (Street, Route, or P.O. Box)	City, State, or Province	Zip/Postal Code

CHURCH INFORMATION

Church Name

Address (Street, Route, or P.O. Box)	City, State, or Province	Zip/Postal Code

CHANGE REQUEST ONLY

☐ Former Name

☐ Former Address	City, State, or Province	Zip/Postal Code

☐ Former Church	City, State, or Province	Zip/Postal Code

Signature of Pastor, Conference Leader, or Other Church Leader	Date

*New participants are requested but not required to give SS# and date of birth. Existing participants, please give CGSP# when using SS# for the first time. Thereafter, only one ID# is required. **Mail to:** Christian Growth Study Plan, 127 Ninth Ave., North, Nashville, TN 37234-0117. Fax: (615)251-5067

Rev. 6-99